MAN & THE UNIVERSE

MAN & THE UNIVERSE

An Islamic Perspective

Mostafa al-Badawi

Revised & Expanded Edition

AWAKENING

PUBLISHED BY THE PRESS SYNDICATE OF AWAKENING PUBLICATIONS
Uplands Business Centre, Bernard Street, Swansea, SA2 ODR, United Kingdom

AWAKENING PUBLICATIONS
Uplands Business Centre, Bernard Street, Swansea, SA2 ODR, United Kingdom
P.O. Box 360009, Milpitas, CA 95036, United States of America

ISBN: 978-1-905837-36-6

First published in 1999 in South Africa
Second Edition published in 2002
Revised and Expanded Edition published in 2010 by Awakening Publications

Typeset in Sabondiactritic

بسم الله الرحمن الرحيم

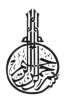

Mostafa al-Badawi is one of the world's premier translators of Islamic spiritual texts. He is a Consultant Psychiatrist and member of the Royal College of Psychiatrists. He studied under many shaykhs, foremost among whom is the late Habib Ahmad Mashhur al-Haddad. His other translations include: *Book of Assistance*, *The Lives of Man*, *Two Treatises*, *The Prophetic Invocations*, *Degrees of the Soul*, and more. He resides in Madinah.

CONTENT

INTRODUCTION IX

I. THE ISLAMIC PERSPECTIVE

1. THE UNIVERSE 3
2. MAN 23
3. THE TIMES 55

II. THE WEST

4. THE INVERTED CIVILIZATION 73

III. NORMATIVE ISLAMIC VALUES

5. WHAT IS A NORM? 95
6. ISLAMIC PSYCHOTHERAPY 129
7. WAR 135

CONCLUSION 149
WORKS CITED 155
INDEX 157

INTRODUCTION

Man, the being most able to know and understand, may rightly be called the consciousness of the universe.

The universe, surrounding him visibly and invisibly, contains the signs and means by which he survives and is enabled to fulfil his potential for knowledge.

God, the Absolute, is that which created the myriad worlds: from the tiniest subatomic particles, to the whirling galaxies, to the invisible worlds with all their beings, levels, and modes. He created what we know and what we do not know. Man has been gifted with an integral intelligence, which, when exercised in accordance with the Absolute's laws, is able to comprehend the cosmic laws governing the Absolute's creation: those defining man's place in it, and those leading to the knowledge of God Himself.

To realize this potential to its fullest and rise from knowledge of the relative to that of the Absolute, man has always been guided by successive Divine messages, delivered by Messengers, who are the most perfect of men, fitted and qualified to receive and transmit this Divine guidance. The Message itself has always been an affirmation of Divine Unity, Transcendence, and Omnipotence, and an invitation to mankind to submit to the Supreme Good and enjoy the consequent benefits.

Those Divine Messengers in possession of a scripture became founders of religions, establishing formal worship of the Absolute and the observation of His sacred law within a particular community or geographic location. Other Divine Envoys were then often sent to reinvigorate religions when their adherents were in danger of either deviating too far from them or of abandoning them altogether.

Religions are always at their purest and most dynamic form within the lifetime of their founders, this time being the summit after which there must be decline. As stated above, decline is delayed by subsequent Prophets, but eventually each religion grows weaker and weaker, then dies.

The laws governing the birth and death of religions, as well as the criteria required to distinguish between living, dying, and dead religions were known to the sages of old. Today this knowledge exists only within the last surviving religion, Islam, and then only within a very small minority of Muslims. The rest of mankind does not even suspect the existence of such knowledge.

As with all other religions, Islam also did not escape gradual deterioration. However, it is the last in revelation and unique in possessing an incorruptible Sacred Book, the Qur'ān. Because of this, Muslims to this day know that they each must live their life, in its smallest and most ordinary details, according to Divine ordinance. And more importantly, they still possess the original sources in which to find clearly delineated patterns of behaviour. They know that the answers to all the questions, great and small, which perplex mankind, are to be found in their Book.

Thus, to speak of man and the universe is, of necessity, to draw on Islamic sources, for only the Islamic perspective retains the full vigour of its God-given wisdom in sum and in detail. Should one seek this kind of knowledge elsewhere one will run into insurmountable problems. Even the most cursory glance at the original sources of other religions will reveal that the distance between them and modern man has become so immense as to render them indecipherable. In addition to this is the historical fact that they have been clearly tampered with and so become full of contradictions.

The original differences between one religion and another appear in their sacred laws, each being prescribed for a particular time and place. Sacred law is that which regulates the relationship between man and his Creator and between one human being and another. These laws, contained in revealed scripture, must thus include patterns of worship and of social interaction.

The last Divine message was sent through the last and most perfect among Divine Messengers, Muḥammad, may the Absolute's blessings and peace be upon him. The message, as all Divine messages, affirms Divine Unity, Transcendence, and Omnipotence. This last sacred scripture is the Qur'ān which, contrary to previous scriptures, has been preserved *verbatim* from the time it was revealed. It is in the unique position of having its integrity guaranteed by the Revealer, the Absolute, till the end of time. And these claims are historically verifiable facts.

This being the case, Muslims are the last repositories of revealed knowledge on this planet and they will remain the treasury of sacred wisdom as long as human beings remain on earth. The Islamic perspective is not and cannot be different from the spirit of the original wisdom which formed the core of every previous revelation. The source of all revelation being one, the essence of all messages is one. However, one has to look beyond form, to perceive meaning thus grasping the underlying unity. Unfortunately modern man has become incapable of doing so.

Since the brutal irruption of the West into the Muslim world around two centuries ago, Muslims have had to face the challenge of living and surviving spiritually in an increasingly hostile environment. Some have coped better than others. The *ʿulamāʾ*, the traditional scholars of Islam, were in the main immune to the influence of alien thought and, with a few notorious exceptions, fought a protracted rearguard battle. The masses, however, whose knowledge of principles was at best elementary, were swept away by the tidal wave of Westernization, losing in the process what little they had possessed. Thus deprived of all means to evaluate what was presented to them as 'scientific' knowledge, the masses were vulnerable to all kinds of subversion. The first to fall prey to this danger were the most 'educated,' namely the politicians, university professors, writers, journalists, doctors and other professionals. These, the worldly elite, were the most vulnerable. Their education gave them a superficial mentality, and their social status a false sense of superiority, of being the forerunners of 'progress' in their countries. These factors submerged whatever sacred knowledge they still possessed and made them the unconscious allies of the colonial forces they thought they were opposing.

Although the nefarious nature of the 'machine' culture has now been sufficiently exposed and many are no longer under its spell, it is too late to attempt a return to a pre-Westernization pattern. Muslims have no option but to take stock of the situation as it now stands and begin from where they are.

The current reaction of the Islamic world against Western materialism and immorality has generated attempts to Islamicise various activities and has led to the emergence of widely divergent opinions as to how best to effect a restoration of Islamic integrity. These opinions range from the so-called fundamentalist outlook, with its superficial view of Islam as a set of rules solely concerned with the purely outward dimensions of religion and thus quite willing to impose or even enforce this set of rules on others, to a modernist outlook disguising itself as Islam. This latter outlook claims that since Islam can be applied at all times and in all places it should accept indiscriminately whatever comes from the West and simply reassign to each thing an Arabic label, as if relabelling would alter its anti-Islamic character. The majority of Muslims, however, are at a loss, unable to decide what to accept or what to reject and on what bases.

The ability to discriminate between that which is Islamically unacceptable and that which may be assimilated without harm must be based on a sound grasp of principles. Unfortunately, most Muslims have now reached the stage where they no longer even know what principles are. The few attempts which have been made in recent years to restate Islamic knowledge in terms understandable to today's mentality have floundered because of this deficiency. Many 'educated' people today feel that the most cursory knowledge of religion gives them the right to speak in its name and in opposition to recognized religious authority. Such people have already committed monumental blunders.

One hears all the time that Islam encourages 'science,' and the relevant *ḥadīth*s[1] are bandied about in the media, but all attempts to clearly define what kind of science the *ḥadīth*s refer to are methodically obstructed and prevented from reaching the public. The suggestion which is constantly put forward in the media, is that by pursuing worldly knowledge at the expense of revealed knowledge one is still complying perfectly with the Prophetic *ḥadīth*s in question.

This has become so commonplace that, whereas in previous times the term *ʿālim* could only be applied to a religious scholar, it has now come to be applied almost exclusively to an expert in modern science. The chasm between the doctrine of Islam and its

1. A *ḥadīth* is a Prophetic tradition, an utterance of the Prophet ﷺ.

practical consequences is being deliberately expanded all the time. The kind of reasoning needed to deduce, for instance, from the doctrine of God's Unity that one ought to love one's brother seems to be beyond the reach of most people now.

A small minority of Muslims have been able to join to the currently approved Western education a sufficiently profound knowledge of religion to initiate the much-needed restatement of Islamic principles in today's language. For example, the few attempts made in recent years to formulate an Islamic psychology, a task necessary for the definition of man, have yet to reach any degree of profundity. Most of what has been written so far amounts to no more than collections of quotations from the Qur'ān and *ḥadīth*s concerning the soul (*nafs*) or the heart (*qalb*), which neither organize this knowledge nor draw conclusions. Other writings more or less restate Western theory in Islamic terminology. There is a clear lack of drawing from traditional sources, perhaps because of the writers' inability to understand these sources on their own terms, or even because of their ignorance of the existence of such sources and their belief that psychology is something invented by the West. The same goes for sociology, politics, theories of history, and so on. There is little point in going into the history of Islamic psychology, except to say that it has been formulated in detail by leading scholars such as Imām al-Ghazālī[2] or philosophers such as Ibn Sīnā (Avicenna).[3] The vocabularies of these schools differ and there are terms borrowed from Greek, however, both are careful ultimately to confine their expositions to that which is entirely compatible with revealed principles.

2. Imām Abū Ḥāmid al-Ghazālī (D. 505 AH/1111 CE), known as the 'Proof of Islam,' was the foremost scholar of his time and who still influences Islamic thinking and scholarship to this day. He is the author of the famous *Iḥyā' ʿUlūm al-Dīn* (*Revival of Religious Sciences*).]

3. Ibn Sīnā was the foremost Peripatetic philosopher in Islam, as well as one of the world's most famous physicians (D. 432 AH /1037 CE).

A principle is that which properly depends on nothing outside itself and upon which other things depend, or that from which things derive and which is itself derived from nothing. Strictly speaking, the only Principle is God. However, taken in a more relative sense, the term may be used to denote universal and immutable laws from which other more limited laws derive, which will in turn become principles for even more limited laws. The lower the level, the less unchanging and the more restricted the meaning becomes.

No theory may have real validity unless it is based on principles derived from revelation. There can be no exception to this rule because these principles are universal and must govern the study of any science, however grossly material it may be. This is the only way to guarantee sufficient objectivity in any branch of knowledge and to prevent its contamination by human bias and the unforeseen calamities that may arise from its resultant misapplication. The Qur'ān states, *A good word is as a good tree: its roots are firm, and its branches are in heaven; it gives its produce every season by the leave of its Lord* (14:24). The roots or principles are firm because they sprout from the Divine word, and its produce is therefore abundant and healthy. In contrast, without such firm implantation the tree would be rootless and thus unstable, unhealthy and unlikely to be of any profit: *The likeness of a corrupt word is as a corrupt tree, uprooted from the earth, lacking stability* (14:26).

The purpose of this book is to define man in relation to the universe. It must therefore offer the reader the Islamic doctrine concerning the structure of both man and the universe, and it must situate man in time and space, both as an individual and within his social context. This should afford the frame of reference against which empirical knowledge can then be measured and evaluated.

The definition of the human situation according to the Islamic perspective should be of value to Muslims and non-Muslims alike.

Muslim psychologists, psychiatrists and other mental health professionals, sociologists, anthropologists, historians, and others, should find herein the necessary doctrinal framework on which to establish Islamic theory and practice, while their non-Muslim colleagues should find in it a stimulating perspective going much deeper than anything they are used to. There is nothing very technical about this book, and the message it contains is universal. The general reader, especially westernized Muslims and non-Muslims interested in traditional spirituality, should find in this brief but comprehensive exposition of Islamic doctrine the answer to many of the questions of the age. It must be clearly stated at the outset, however, that a book of this size can hardly do justice to such a vast subject. Therefore, once he has grasped the basic ideas in the book, the interested reader will have to make additional efforts in order to enlarge his understanding of each area and gain the necessary proficiency to be able to apply such knowledge practically. The help of a qualified teacher is almost always required in such matters.

The knowledge contained in this book has been drawn from the most authoritative sources; it is entirely based on the Qur'ān and *ḥadīth*. In such an endeavor there is no room for individual opinion, and conjecture is expressly forbidden, especially with regard to principles; but where the details of practical applications are concerned, much more latitude is allowed. Therefore, since the book deals mainly with principles, none of it constitutes my own theorizing. The hierarchical arrangement of the virtues in the chapter on virtues and vices is admittedly rather idiosyncratic, this being the result of the quest for conceptual simplicity, but the definition and relevance of the virtues themselves are entirely traditional. I have drawn extensively on the work of Imām al-Ghazālī, partly because he undertook in his time precisely the task that needs to be repeated today. He mastered the Greek philosophers and other schools of relevance in his day, subjected them to rigorous critical analysis, retained whatever he found consistent with revealed criteria and discarded the rest.

Textual evidence for the subjects under discussion is almost limitless since the function of religion is indeed to define man in relation to his environment, then instruct him on how to live in the best possible manner in such an environment. Had we wished to produce an exhaustive account, the book would have easily run into several volumes. However, the intention was simply to attract attention to the principles in question in order to stimulate other minds to elaborate on them and discuss explicitly much which remains implicit here.

MOSTAFA AL-BADAWI

PART ONE

The Islamic Perspective

1. THE UNIVERSE

DIMENSIONS OF EXISTENCE

God is Absolute; all else is relative. This means that only He is Real; all else, in reality, being dependent upon Him. It also means that only He is Free, all else being subject to constraints of various kinds and degrees. God is Infinite; all else is limited.

God is Transcendent: He is not only beyond all limits of time, space, form, or change; but beyond all conceivable limits, and beyond all description.

The first thing that He created was pure light, or pure spirit, which amounts to the same thing. From that He created the rest of the universe in a descending hierarchy wherein the lower the realm, the more limited and opaque it becomes.

Our visible world, as well as other (to us) invisible worlds, take their contingent existences and reality from God. Higher, invisible worlds have their own purposes and realities just as our material realm does. All of creation is, of course, an interconnected whole, created by and entirely dependent on God; yet in relation to each other, each realm of existence is dependent on and a shadow of the realm above it, right up to the Attributes of God and, beyond that, God Himself, Exalted is He, Who can only be truly known by Himself. The higher the realm of existence, the 'nearer' to God it is, as it were, the more 'real' it becomes and the less conditioned it is in relation to whatever is below it. The 'normal' everyday world we believe we live and function in is affected immeasurably by the realities above it, whether we are aware of this or not. Knowledge of the invisible domains is not conjectural but based on scriptural evidence given to mankind by Divine revelation. More importantly, these domains are within the direct perception of Divine Messengers and other illumined beings, who can see, hear, smell, and describe them from firsthand experience. This knowledge recedes into the background and then disappears as people become more materialistic and opaque; however, without it, an adequate understanding of the human situation is impossible.

According to tradition, our world, the material domain, when compared with the surrounding subtle domain, is no larger than a mother's womb in relation to the whole of planet Earth. One's escape from the constraints of this world at death and release into the relative freedom of the Intermediary Realm is thus comparable to one's previous escape from the constraint of the womb and release into the relative freedom of the terrestrial world. Just as for a foetus or a new-born infant the whole of our world must necessarily seem full of fantastic, incomprehensible forms and relationships that may only be comprehended through guided experience and study, so initially, for us, the realities of the higher realms may also seem fantastic and incomprehensible. They are, however, clear, distinguishable and usable; and their meaning and function become apparent through study and guidance.

It is said that God's universe is made of eighteen thousand worlds, one of the smallest of which is the material or visible domain (*ʿālam al-shahāda* or *ʿālam al-mulk*): the observable cosmos with its billions of galaxies, its unimaginable intergalactic distances, its pulsars, quasars, novas and black holes. This domain is contained within the Terrestrial Heaven (*al-samāʾ al-dunyā*), and represents no more than a grain of sand in the desert in relation to the invisible domain (*ʿālam al-ghayb* or *ʿālam al-malakūt*). The latter is composed of seven superimposed heavens surrounded by the Divine Footstool (*al-kursī*), which is itself contained by the Divine Throne (*al-ʿarsh*). *His Footstool contains the heavens and the earth*, declares the Qurʾān (2:255). More precisions are given in a *ḥadīth*.

The seven heavens and the seven earths compared with the Footstool are no more than a ring cast in the wilderness; and the superiority of the Throne over the Footstool is again like that of the wilderness over the ring.[4]

At the center of the seventh heaven is the Populous House (*al-bayt al-maʿmūr*), said in *ḥadīth*s to be the heavenly sanctuary visited daily by seventy thousand angels, and which corresponds to the Kaʿba[5] in the material dimension. The connection between the Kaʿba and *al-bayt al-maʿmūr* is uninterrupted, since there are corresponding sanctuaries at the centre of each of the other heavens, each being the shadow cast by the one immediately superior to it. The sanctuary in the Terrestrial Heaven is termed the House of Might (*bayt al-ʿizza*). This is where the Qurʾān was caused to descend on the Night of Destiny (*laylat al-qadr*), before being revealed portion by portion to the

Prophet ﷺ over the twenty-three years from the beginning of his mission and the first revelation in the cave of Ḥirā in Makka to

---

4 Ibn Ḥibbān *Ṣaḥīḥ*, 2/77; Ibn Kathīr, *Tafsīr*, 1/311, 587.

5. The Kaʿba is the Sacred House of God erected by Abraham in Makka. The Sanctuary is the House together with the area around it, declared forbidden by Abraham, may peace be upon him. Human beings and wild animals and plants are inviolable in the Sanctuary. To carry weapons with the intention of fighting is forbidden and non-believers are not allowed to enter.

his death in Madīna. The image of this house in the material world is the stone Kaʿba, the location upon which alight 'one hundred and twenty mercies at each instant, sixty for those who are circling around it, forty for those who are praying [before it], and twenty for those who are gazing at it.'[6]

In the seventh heaven is the Lote Tree of the Limit (*sidrat al-muntahā*) said in *ḥadīth* to be 'near the Throne and so immense that a rider may travel under the shade of one of its branches for a hundred years.'[7] It marks the limit of that knowledge which may be bestowed on created beings, whether human or otherwise. The Footstool is the pedestal upon which rest not only the King's throne but also His two feet.[8]

God uses symbols to refer to His Attributes, since they would otherwise be impossible to describe. Only the densest minds are tempted to take symbols literally, and only superficial minds brush them aside by labeling them myths, rather than trying to penetrate the veil and receive their meaning. In this context, the two feet symbolize the complementarity of the Divine Attributes of Beauty and Majesty as manifested in the domain contained within the Footstool, namely, the heavens and the earth. This is related to the two Divine hands mentioned in the Qur'ān where God reproaches the Devil for disobeying the Divine command to prostrate himself before Adam, may peace be upon him: *What has prevented you from prostrating yourself before that [which] I have created with My two hands?* (38:75). The 'two hands' are to be interpreted as the hand of Compassion and the hand of Might or Compulsion, which represent the Attributes of Beauty and Majesty. One hand bestowed upon Adam his higher angelic or spiritual nature, while the other

6. Ṭabarānī, *al-Muʿjam al-Kabīr*, 11/195.

7. Tirmidhī, KITĀB ṢIFAT AL-JANNA, 9; al-Ḥakim, *al-Mustadrak*, 2/469.

8. Al-Ḥakim, *al-Mustadrak*, 2/282; Ibn Kathīr, *Tafsīr*, 1/310.

gave him his lower or animal nature. The first hand bestowed upon him qualities such as compassion, gentleness, generosity and affability; the second qualities such as dignity, firmness and courage. There is another passage where the two hands are again mentioned: *No! His two hands are wide open* (5:64). They are interpreted by the commentators as together representing Infinite Generosity: one of them bestows upon all creatures the good of this world, and the other that of the next. Again, one hand grants outward gifts, and the other, inward ones. The same is implied by the *ḥadīth*, 'The heart of the believer lies between two of the All-Merciful's fingers.[9] These two fingers turn the heart either toward faith or disbelief, toward attachment to the higher spiritual world or the lower material worlds, toward the remembrance of God or toward distraction, and so on. Thus understood, the two fingers clearly represent Mercy and Wrath.

Beyond the Footstool lies the Throne, the level in which the Attribute of Total Mercy or *Raḥmāniyya* manifests itself: *The All-Merciful (al-Raḥmān) has established Himself on the Throne* (20:5). There the vengeful Attributes are no longer manifest; all is compassion and contentment. The Throne is the roof of Paradise where all is bliss.

It should be remembered that the invisible domain is not spatially conditioned, and that the use of spatial imagery in the representation of higher realities such as the Throne, the Footstool and the Lote Tree, is simply a means of expressing in human language what would otherwise be incommunicable. There are obvious drawbacks in using such imagery, one of the most important being that two different descriptions of one and the same reality may seem incompatible. For example, as the Throne is usually understood as something that surrounds and contains, one of its names is therefore *al-ʿarsh al-muḥīṭ*, the Surrounding Throne. The same Throne is described elsewhere as the centre of the created universe, the seat of the Spirit (*al-*

9. Muslim, KITĀB AL-QADAR, 17; Ibn Māja, KITĀB AL-DUʿĀ', 2.

rūḥ) and of the Supreme Assembly (*al-mala' al-aᶜlā*). It is only when the Throne is viewed as being at the centre that the Lote Tree and the Populous House may be said to be in its proximity. The two viewpoints are given simultaneously in the following passage: *The Throne bearers and those around it hymn the praises of their Lord and believe in Him, and ask forgiveness for the believers: Our Lord, You have encompassed everything in your Mercy and Knowledge.* (40:7)

Here the Throne is said to be borne by the bearers, but there are those who are around it, that is, around the centre. At the same time, the Divine Mercy, which is established 'on' the Throne is said to encompass everything, so the Throne must clearly be peripheral and not central. This one example shows that such descriptions of higher realities should not be taken literally, and that a symbol resembles the reality it indicates in some ways and necessarily differs in others. Just as it is for the invisible domains, the realities of these symbols are witnessed directly and experienced after death, or as a gift from God to those whom He draws near, such as the Prophet and those who follow faithfully in his footsteps.

To remain within the realm of things unfamiliar to most of today's Muslims, and having mentioned the Supreme Assembly, let us recall that when the Prophet ﷺ was given the choice between prolonging his life on earth or returning to his Lord, he was heard to murmur, 'O God! The Supreme Company! (*al-rafīq al-aᶜlā*).'[10] This Supreme Company or Assembly is said by many authorities to be made up of the Spirit (*al-rūḥ*), the four great Archangels, Gabriel, Michael, Seraphiel (Isrfīl) and Azrael, and the spirits of the Prophets, surrounded by the Throne bearers and other angels. 'When God passes a decree,' says the *ḥadīth*,

> the bearers of the Throne glorify Him, then those in the heaven be-

10. Bukhārī, KITĀB AL-MARDA', 19, and KITĀB FAḌĀ'IL AL-ṢAḤĀBA, 5; Muslim, KITĀB AL-SALĀM, 46.

neath them, then those beneath them, until the glorifications reach those who dwell in thisTerrestrial Heaven. Then those around the bearers of the Throne ask them, 'What has your Lord said?' and they inform them, and the dwellers of the heavens question each other until news reaches the dwellers of this heaven.[11]

Spanning these levels is the Intermediary Realm (*al-barzakh*), where the spirits abide at death after their departure from this world. It is said to have the shape of an inverted horn, the narrowest part beginning in the infra-human invisible domain and ending in *Sijjīn*, the abode of the disbelievers and hypocrites, while the widest part is *ᶜIlliyūn*, the roof of which is the Throne. The spirits also exist in this horn prior to their descent into this world, and after their return there they remain until the resurrection. Compared with the material world, the *barzakh* is subtle, whereas compared with the higher dimensions, it is dense.

In these worlds, abstract things take on forms, much in the same way as abstract meanings and formless realities take on forms or images to appear in dreams. Certain Sūras (chapters) from the Qur'ān, for instance, appear as light in the grave, or as clouds at the Resurrection, shading those who used to recite them during their earthly lives. Evil deeds also appear to those who perpetrated them, taking the form of huge venomous snakes, scorpions, or scorching fires. Then there are the Scales upon which deeds will be weighed. These deeds must therefore take on substance to be weighed, and they may be outweighed by a small parchment inscribed with *Lā ilāha illa'llāh* (there is no God but Allah). The appearance of abstract meanings in perceptible forms is called *ᶜālam al-mithāl*, the World of Similitudes. These similitudes may even appear within the material dimension, as when Gabriel appeared to Mary: ... *he appeared to her in the form of a well-made human* (19:17).

11. Muslim, KITĀB AL-SALĀM, 134; Tirmidhī, KITĀB AL-TAFSĪR, Sura 34.

The word used in this passage is *tamaththala*, which means that Gabriel took on the likeness or the similitude of a man. This is the nature of the Intermediary Realm, of the human imagination and of dreams. The world of imagination (*ʿālam al-khayāl*) and that of dreams correspond inwardly to what the World of Similitudes is outwardly. In this fact lies the explanation of the strange happenings that the dead experience in their graves, for they are not spatially contained in the narrow sandy pit where the body is deposited, but rather in the surrounding subtle dimension.

Another invisible world is that of the jinn, the fiery creatures who, being endowed with reason, are free to accept or reject Divine messages and are thus divided, as humans are, into believers and disbelievers. The latter are the followers of the Devil and carry out his subversive plans. The worst among them are called demons. The root from which the word 'jinn' is derived signifies hidden, invisible or covered. *Junūn*, or madness, is derived from the same root, not because madness is due to the jinn, but because madness is defined as that which 'covers' reason and hides it: *junna ʿaqluhu* means, 'his reason has become hidden.' The jinn are capable of appearing in, and interacting with, the material dimension, for they are made of energy, much like the kinds of energy known to physical science. There are also levels in the adjacent subtle domain which constitute the medium through which such phenomena as magic and sorcery (*siḥr*), the evil eye (*ḥasad*), and hypnosis exercise their action.

The created universe is a single closely interconnected whole. Whatever happens in one dimension has repercussions throughout the hierarchy. The visible and invisible worlds are in constant interaction, both for good and for evil. The effect of faith and virtuous behaviour is to unlock the gates between this world and the higher ones and to shut the gates between it and the lower ones. The result is the presence of *baraka*, the spiritual influence or benediction that comes from above and pervades everything, outwardly and inwardly, to make it flourish:

> *Had the People of the Book [Jews and Christians] believed and feared God, We would have acquitted them of their sins and admitted them to gardens of bliss. Had they upheld the Torah and the Gospel, and what was revealed to them from their Lord, they would have eaten both from above them and from below their feet.* (5:65-66)

> *Had the people of the cities believed and feared God, We would have opened upon them blessings* (barakāt) *from the sky and from the earth.* (7:96)

The reference in both these passages is to rainfall and the crops it causes to grow. The *baraka* which is the result of strong faith, virtuous behaviour and sincere prayers makes both rain and crops plentiful. The opposite also occurs as a result of the opposite kind of behaviour. Misery and destruction befall the corrupt as a result of what they do:

> *Corruption has appeared in the land and sea, for that men's own hands have earned, that He may let them taste some part of that which they have done, that they may return. Say: 'Journey in the land, then see how was the end of those that were before; most of them were idolaters.'* (30:41-42)

This, however, is a highly complex matter involving a great many factors of which the ones we have just mentioned are but a few. Another element to take into account is the Divine law whereby whoever does good receives his reward in this world. Disbelievers who work hard at tilling their land will reap their reward in the form of satisfactory crops, although the end result of their whole way of life cannot but be catastrophic. Likewise, believers who neglect their land will inevitably see their crops fail. The mitigating presence of saintly persons among a corrupt population is a compensatory factor of substantial weight, due to the power of their *baraka* that, unknown to the community at large, neutralizes to a certain extent the adverse effects of corruption.

The invisible worlds also exercise their influence at the individual level. There is a two-way traffic between each person and the higher and lower worlds. For instance, there is a well-known *ḥadīth* to the effect that whenever a person utters *Lā ilāha illa'llāh*, a pillar of light extending upward all the way to the Divine Presence begins to resonate and continues to do so until the command issues from that Presence for it to stop, to which it replies that it cannot possibly stop unless the person in question is forgiven all his sins.[12] Other good deeds also ascend to the Throne, they are noted by the Supreme Assembly, who bless and support those whose deeds gain their approval and satisfaction. The corrupt, on the other hand, are cursed and obstructed in their endeavours. Again, the result of such action by the Supreme Assembly is not to eradicate all evil, nor will the people they support always be perceptibly victorious in this world. Evil is a necessity and the times must deteriorate so as to reach the bottom of the abyss, at which time the Horn will be sounded and the Resurrection begin.

There are also subversive influences arising from the lower infernal regions. The Qur'ān states, concerning Satan and his host: *He sees you, he and his tribe, from whence you see them not. We made the devils allies for those who do not believe* (7:27). Also: *Shall I tell you on whom the devils come down? They come down on every sinful slanderer* (26:221); and: *The devils inspire their allies to dispute with you* (6:121). It is also written in the Qur'ān: *Those who have said: 'God is our Lord,' then were steadfast, upon them the angels descend [saying]: 'Fear not, neither sorrow, and rejoice in that garden that you were promised. We are your allies in this world and the next ...'* (41:30).

12. Abū Nuʿaym, *Ḥilyat al-Awliyā'*, 3/164; al-Mundhirī, *al-Targhīb wa'l- Tarhīb*, 2/269; al-Haytamī, *Majmaʿ al-Zawā'id*, 10/82.

THE PAIRS

And of each thing created We two pairs, says the Qur'ān (51:49); thus it is to be understood that everything in creation is paired. The Divine Attributes are also said to be paired, for God is *Dhū'l-Jalālī wa'l-Ikrām* (the Possessor of Majesty and Generosity). Only the Divine Essence (*al-Dhāt*) is unique: *Say: He, God is Unique* (112:1). This is one reason why the Qur'ān affirms Divine Transcendence, God's uniqueness and incomparability, before mentioning the pairs, both those we know and those we do not: *Transcendent is the Creator of all the pairs, of what the earth produces, of themselves, and of what they do not know* (36:36). This is reaffirmed in other passages such as the following: *The Originator of the heavens and the earth; He has made for you, of yourselves, pairs, and pairs also of the cattle, multiplying you therein. Like Him there is naught* (42:11). Here God speaks of Himself in His aspect as Originator, then He mentions the pairs, the heavens and the earth, which are the subtle cosmic and material dimensions. He then mentions at the terrestrial level the human and animal male/female pairs, and then reaffirms His transcendence, Like Him there is naught. Examples of pairs from every conceivable perspective can be found in the Qur'ān. From the structural or static cosmic perspective we can take as an example the heavens/earth pair, which may also be termed visible/invisible, or *mulk/malakūt*.

These, from the sequential perspective, correspond to this world/next world, or *dunya/ākhira*. The next world is further divided into Paradise/Hell, felicity/wretchedness. Then within the terrestrial world we have day/night, winter/summer, sun/moon, mountains/plains, land/sea, then the vegetable, animal, and human pairs. At the individual level we have knowledge/ignorance, vice/virtue, love/hate, fortitude/panic, remembrance of God/distraction, attachment to the world/detachment, and so on. Similar relationships will be found at the molecular, atomic and subatomic levels.

To render these relationships clear we must know that everything in existence was made according to a model or archetype in the eternal, immutable Divine knowledge. Every relationship here below corresponds to another at a higher level, and so on until their origin in the uncreated Divine knowledge. The first pair, which was created expressing this duality and which became the model for every subsequent pair, is that of the Pen (*Qalam*) and the Guarded Tablet (*al-Lawḥ al-Maḥfūẓ*). The first is active and represents Majesty, and the second is passive in relation to it and represents Beauty. The Prophet ﷺ said that the first thing that God created was the Pen, that He then made the Tablet, then the Pen was commanded to inscribe on the Tablet God's knowledge concerning His creation from the beginning to the Last Day.[13] Thus the Pen actively wrote and the Tablet passively received its imprint. The first human pair was also of an active pole, Adam, who was first to be created, and Eve, his passive complement.

The terms active/passive, male/female, positive/negative are always to be understood in a relative and not absolute sense, since what is active in relation to one thing is at the same time passive in relation to another. The Pen, active in relation to the Tablet, is also eminently passive in relation to the Divine command which moves it. Men are active, which in this context means protective and supportive, in relation to their wives, but passive in relation to their parents, teachers and superiors; whereas women are passive in relation to their husbands, which means accepting of their protection and support, but active in relation to their children, whether males or females. Within a single relationship, for instance that of the student and teacher, in general the student is passive in relation to the teacher but there may be some psychological elements in the student

13. Tirmidhī, KITĀB AL-TAFSĪR, Sura 68.

which are active in relation to other particular elements in the teacher. Thus each pole of a dyad not only has the potential for the opposite role in another dyad, but can also be part of a complex set of relationships where active and passive interactions exist in both directions. The reason for this is that each pole of a dyad carries within it some of the constituents of the other, an obvious example being the fact that both males and females produce male and female hormones, which differ only in their relative quantities. Furthermore the term 'passive' denotes no weakness or imperfection. The Divine Attributes of Beauty constitute passive perfection, whereas those of Majesty constitute active perfection. Active and passive attributes or roles in earthly creatures are but the earthly shadows of these Divine perfections. Passive attributes are no less necessary than active ones, for each complements the other.

The two poles of a dyad may belong to the same degree of existence or to two superimposed degrees, in other words there are 'horizontal' as well as 'vertical' relationships. When a relationship is vertical, the higher pole is always predominantly active in relation to the lower one. To take the human being for example, the soul or psyche is higher than the body, and thus in the psyche/soma pair, it is predominantly active. In relation to the spirit, however, the soul is lower and thus chiefly passive.[14] To take a cosmic example, the Divine Throne is active in relation to the Footstool, which in turn is mostly active in relation to the seven heavens beneath it, which in turn are mainly active in relation to the material world. The active/passive relationship of the pairs may, at the lowest levels, be considered one of opposition, as in good/evil for instance. In most instances, however, it will be one of complementarity rather than opposition, and this applies more pervasively the higher the level.

---

14. For a definition of the Soul and the Spirit, refer to Chapter 2, 'Spirit and Soul,' below.

Also to be mentioned in this context are the arrangements of multidyadic relationships in complex interacting systems. This perspective has been partly studied by modern systems theorists with some relatively valid conclusions put forth, although they are limited by the very nature of material science. Each system is conceived as composed of smaller systems and forming part of a larger one. These systems within systems are in equilibrium. Every equilibrium is likely to be periodically disrupted, only to be replaced by a new balance after a period of disequilibrium, which is to say that every equilibrium is relative and carries within it the seed of future disequilibrium. Within each system the lighter or more passive components are conceived of as orbiting the heavier or more active components. This may be literal, as in the case of electrons and protons and suns and planets, or it may be less evident as when applied at the social or individual levels. In a tribal setting the members of each clan may be seen as moving within the orbit of the clan's chieftain, whose authority is the main centripetal force within the clan. Each chieftain is moving within the larger orbit of the tribal chief, who is thus the centre of gravity of the whole tribe. In this context, the centrifugal forces will be each tribesman's egoistic desires and tendency to prefer his own wishes over the communal good of the tribe. At the family level, the members are subject to the centripetal pull of the head of the family; the dispersing centrifugal forces will be each member's perception of his self-interest as incongruent with that of the family. Intrapsychically, the soul's elements may easily be conceived of as orbiting around the centre of gravity, that is the heart. We shall discuss this in more detail in the chapter concerned with the soul and the spirit. It suffices to say here that these elements are also subject to centripetal unifying and centrifugal dispersing influences. This is why the Qur'ān speaks of those possessed of a 'core' (*lubb*), that is a unifying centre of consciousness. For the power of the soul lies in the harmonizing of all of its elements so as to remove inner conflict, work against distraction and the dispersal of attention in order to unite the soul in the drive to reach immutable truth. This is inner unification, or *tawḥīd*. The Qur'ān states:

> *Surely in the creation of the heavens and the earth and in the alternation of night and day there are signs for those possessed of cores [centred minds] who remember God standing, sitting, and on their sides, and reflect upon the creation of the heavens and earth: 'Our Lord, You have not created this in vain, Transcendent are You, so preserve us from the torment of the fire.'* (3:190-91)

These people, possessed of centred minds, are those who practise the remembrance of God uninterruptedly, which is here expressed by their doing it in all possible postures: standing, sitting, and on their sides. Thus they defeat all dispersing tendencies and win inner harmony or unity. At the highest level, whether spiritually, within, or cosmically, without, all complementary pairs must resolve into unity.

TIME

Time as we know it is the succession of cyclical events in space. The rotation of the earth on its own axis, its revolving around the sun, and that of the moon around the earth, as well as the observable motion of the constellations allow us to measure time in days, months, years, seasons and other smaller or larger units as may suit various purposes. This is terrestrial time, which is one of the conditions of the material world, another condition being space.[15] Beyond the material world, time and space do not exist. Scholars have always made a distinction between time (*zamān*) and duration (*madda*), time being one of the modes of duration. Duration is what permits the successive unfolding of events. In worlds other than that contained within the Terrestrial Heaven, duration has other indicators:

15. Other conditions implied by space are form and density.

witness the *ḥadīth* stating that the people of the Garden will meet with their Lord face to face at a determined location every Friday. There must therefore be in the Garden something that corresponds with terrestrial time and space, although this will differ from terrestrial conditions as much as the pure, luminous paradisiacal environment differs from the dense, muddy terrestrial one.

The successive unfolding of events within duration is termed by Muslim scholars, chronological succession (*tatabuʿ zamānī*). There is another kind of succession which precedes the creation of both duration and time; this is what the Qur'ān refers to as the 'six days' in which the creation of the world took place. This kind of succession is termed logical succession (*tatabuʿ ʿaqlī*). These events are conceived of as a succession for the sake of intelligibility and because chronological succession at lower levels corresponds to this higher mode of succession. The real implication is, however, that they are stages in the creation process that take place simultaneously.

There is no common measure between earthly time and duration in the higher worlds. This is expressed in the Qur'ān as follows: *To Him the angels and the Spirit ascend in a day, the measure of which is fifty thousand years* (70:2). He directs the affair from heaven to earth, it then ascends to Him in a day, *the measure of which is as a thousand years of your counting* (32:5). *A day with your Lord is as a thousand years of your counting* (22:47).

There is thus time which is outward and objective in the material dimension, duration of different modes in the other worlds, and inward subjective time, which is our waking perception of time and that of the dreamer. Our perception of time is far from uniform, hours of pleasure pass lightly and are perceived as minutes, while minutes of suffering or even simply boredom pass like hours. At the Resurrection the corrupt will be asked how long they have remained on earth and they will answer: *We have remained but a day or part of a day* (3:112), and they will be so convinced of the truth of this that they will add: Ask then the numberers, or the angels who keep count. The Day of Judgement itself will be experienced by the sincere believers as no more than the time taken on earth to pray two prayer cycles (*rakʿa*s) and by others as progressively longer until, for the hypocrites and the worst disbelievers, it will be experienced as fifty thousand years.

Time expands and contracts, becoming lighter in the first instance and denser in the second. The lighter it is, the more *baraka* there is in it and the more that can be achieved in it; whereas the denser it becomes, the less *baraka* it contains and the more obstructive to achievement it becomes. The obvious example of an occasion when time was greatly expanded is the Night Journey of the Prophet, may God's blessings and peace be upon him. On that night he travelled from Makka to Jerusalem, alighting in various locations at Gabriel's bidding to pray. At the Jerusalem Temple he led the other Prophets in prayer, then ascended through the seven heavens to the Throne, the Lote Tree of the Limit, and the meeting with his Lord. He met with various Prophets at each stage of the ascent and had detailed visions of the Garden and the Fire. Yet when he returned to Makka, the bed he had left had not had time to lose its warmth.

There is no difficulty conceiving of variations in inward subjective time, for in dreams and other inner experiences one may travel vast distances and do a great number of things only to find that these experiences took minutes of outward time. As we have shown, outward time is also not uniform since it contracts and expands, thickens and thins, and revolves in cycles. What is it then which indicates these changes? Surely it is not the clock that keeps ticking regularly, but the content of the minutes and hours, that is, the number and size of events occurring within the same objective time. The less obstructive the quality of time, the more one is allowed to do.

Time is manipulated by the Divine power for various purposes, as demonstrated for instance in the story of ʿUzayr, may peace be upon him, in the Qur'ān (2:259) and in the story of the sleepers in the cave (18:8). ʿUzayr died and was revived a hundred years later to find that whereas time had its normal effect on his animal, of which nothing but bones remained, it had been suspended for both himself and his food, neither of which showed the slightest sign of decomposition. As for the sleepers in the cave, they were made to sleep for three hundred and nine years, their vital functions preserved but their consciousness selectively suspended. There are many more examples found in *ḥadīth* and the lives of the Companions of the Prophet Muḥammad, their Followers and other men of God.

Apart from such extraordinary events, certain times are said to be more charged with *baraka*. Such, for example, are the day of ʿArafat each year during the ḥajj pilgrimage, Friday each week, and the last third of the night, the times between the dawn (*subḥ*) prayer and sunrise, and between the afternoon (*ʿaṣr*) prayer and sunset each day. As the Last Day draws nearer, time contracts, thickens, and becomes less conducive to good works. *Baraka* diminishes by the day until none shall remain and the last man of God dies leaving no successor. This will herald the end of terrestrial time and the advent of the Hour. A *ḥadīth* states explicitly, 'The Hour will not arrive until time contracts, so that a year becomes as a month, a month as a week, a week as a day, a day as an hour, and an hour as a fiery flare.'[16] Another *ḥadīth* indicates that time should not be conceived of as linear, as most people tend to think, but rather as circular, or more accurately as spiral, 'Time has turned full circle and returned to what it was when God created the heavens and the earth.'[17] Thus spoke the Prophet ﷺ on the Farewell Pilgrimage. The

16. Tirmidhī, KITĀB AL-ZUHD, 34; Ibn Māja, KITĀB AL-FITAN, 33.

17. Bukhārī, KITĀB BAD' AL-KHALQ, 3.

meaning of this *ḥadīth* is that the configuration of the physical heavens of our world had returned to what it was at the beginning of creation, that time had therefore turned full circle, and that the end was imminent.

2. MAN

THE DESTINY OF MAN

Having deliberately narrowed his horizons to only the material dimension, modern man conceives of himself as a 'thing' that begins at birth, ends at death, and, apart from the pursuit of worldly pleasures, is entirely purposeless. Such intellectual myopia is the inevitable result of his ignorance or denial of the 'before' and 'after' of his earthly life and of his invisible extensions in the subtle and spiritual dimensions. Such knowledge was made available to mankind through Divine revelation, and without it no adequate understanding of the meaning and purpose of man is possible: neither can any decisions be made as to how best to conduct one's life nor can due importance be assigned to any of its sectors. Every single thought or act in a man's life has repercussions in the subtle domains and thus affects his life to come. When a man becomes aware of this fact, his thinking, his system of values and priorities, and his planning differ radically from those of a man who thinks he has only this life to be concerned about and is consequently under considerable unrelenting pressure to gratify as much of his material and social wishes within as short a time as is possible. For convenience of description, man's existence has been divided by Muslim scholars into five stages: pre-earthly, earthly, life in the Intermediary Realm, Resurrection and Judgment, and final abode. It must be well understood that there is no discontinuity between succeeding stages, for as one dies, or exits from the world he lives in, he is instantaneously reborn into the next: birth and death being two sides of the same coin. That which appears as death on one side will appear as birth from the other.

The phenomenon of sleep provides the best example for understanding this, since a man asleep appears to the onlooker to be unconscious and still, when at the same time he may be dreaming vividly. Seen from the outside he appears to exhibit no signs of life apart from breathing, yet inwardly he is living intense and sometimes highly meaningful experiences. This is called the 'little death,' when the senses withdraw from the physical realm. The Qur'ān utilizes the same term for both sleep and death, and also for any other kind of passage from this to the higher worlds: *God takes* (yatawaffā) *the souls at the time of their death, and that which has not died in its sleep; He withholds that against which He has decreed death and releases the others till a stated term. Surely in that are signs for people who reflect* (9:42).

The same word, *yatawaffā*, is used for the action of the Angel of Death when he takes lives, and again for the passage of Jesus, may peace be upon him, from the visible to the invisible world: *I was a witness over them as long as I remained among them, but when You did take me* (tawaffaytanī) *to Yourself, You were the witness over them* (5:117).

The passage from the pre-earthly to the earthly world, that is, the descent of the spirit into the embryo at the one hundred and twentieth day of pregnancy, followed at term by birth, induces in most cases a total forgetfulness of the spirit's previous existence.

This is one of the reasons why so little is known about the pre-earthly stage. Another reason is that, being forced to begin our journey to God from the point where we now stand, it is of no great consequence to know the details of the previous stages. We have to take stock of the situation as it is and act according to the instructions given in the Qur'ān and Sunna[18] which are amply sufficient. The Qur'ān rarely mentions this stage, and very succinctly when it does: *And when your Lord took from the Children of Adam, from their loins, their seed, and made them testify against themselves. 'Am I not your Lord?' They said, 'Indeed, we testify.' Lest you should say on the Day of Rising, 'Of this we were unaware'* (7:172).

On that day the spirits witnessed the unveiled glory of their Lord and testified that they had done so. They could hardly do otherwise, since they bore witness only to what they actually saw. The implication of that testimony is that it is within man's nature to recognize his Lord, whereas the opposite attitude, that of the atheist or the idolater, is deviant and unjustifiable. The only other allusion in the Qur'ān to that stage is the narration of the oath the Prophets were made to take affirming their subordination to the Seal of Prophecy, may God's blessings and peace be upon them all.

> *And when God took the Prophets' pledge, 'That I have given you of Book and wisdom, then there shall come to you a Messenger confirming what is with you, you shall believe in him and you shall assist him.' He said, 'Do you agree, and do you take My burden on that condition?' They said, 'We do agree!' He said, 'Then bear witness and I shall be with you among the witnesses.'* (3:81)

The importance of being aware of pre-earthly life is that it explains some observable human phenomena. For example, the individual differences in spiritual potential are an observable fact.

18. A *Sunna* is an utterance or act of the Prophet ﷺ. These are preserved in detail and constitute the second sacred source of knowledge for Muslims after the Qur'ān.

Furthermore, some people exhibit at a very early age a degree of spiritual maturity that others reach only after a lifetime of effort. Prophets are born, not made. 'I was a Prophet when Adam was still between water and clay,'[19] said the Prophet ﷺ implying that he was fully aware of his pre-earthly condition. Indeed, many men of God of lesser rank than Prophets have also said as much. Imām ʿAlī, for instance, said that he remembered clearly who stood on his right and whom on his left on the day of Am I not your Lord? There are thus exceptions to the rule that human beings are born without the memory of their previous state.

Another example of the influence pre-earthly events have on earthly life is the spontaneous sympathy or antipathy that one often experiences on first meeting a particular person. The explanation of this is that a meeting has already taken place between the spirits in the pre-earthly world, and the harmony or disharmony which resulted determine the subsequently observed response. This is to be clearly understood from the *ḥadīth* quoted by Imām ʿAlī in answer to ʿUmar ibn al-Khaṭṭāb's question as to why a man meets another and likes or dislikes him without the other having done anything to deserve either. ʿAlī explained that the Prophet, may blessings and peace be upon him, had stated that spirits reacted according to their nature, meaning that those spirits they met with in the spiritual world and found themselves in harmony with by their very nature, they later felt attracted to; while those they met and were discordant with, again by essential incompatibility, they were later repelled.[20] What appears as a man's psychological profile in this world is the result of his essential nature, aptitudes and influences carried through from his pre-earthly life, to which are added his genetic make-up and the modification of this by environmental

19. Bukhārī, KITĀB AL-ADAB, 119; Muslim, KITĀB FAḌĀ'IL AL-ṢAḤĀBA.

20. Bukhārī, KITĀB AL-ANBIYĀ', 3; Muslim, KITĀB AL-BIRR, 159 and 160.

factors. We shall return to this subject in the section on personality.

The second stage, life in this world, may be divided into five sub stages: infancy, childhood, youth, maturity and old age. Each of these differs from the others on a number of counts, determining the particular role or function devolved to each, as well as the mode of carrying this out. A clear account of these is given in Imām al-Ḥaddād's *The Lives of Man.*[21] The complementary role of the male/female, or the predominantly active/passive, or the predominantly positive/negative, and so on, affects the whole spectrum of human roles and activities and results in physical, psychological, social and spiritual differences that must always be taken into account.

Death, the passage from this life into the next, is generally regarded as a painful and undesirable experience, the end of everything and the passage into nothingness. There are many manifest errors in such a conception. To begin with, the moribund person who seems semi-conscious or even comatose is experiencing various events which differ according to his background, religion and prior behavior. The weakening of life in the body is due to the weakening of the spirit's bond with it. Some people will appear serene at the time of death; they may be reassured by spiritual presences and may be looking forward to their escape from this world and passage to freedom on the other side. Others such as the hypocrites and the corrupt will experience extreme terror, since the Angel of Death will appear to them in his terrible aspect, that aspect which precisely reflects their own state. Their whole life is paraded before their eyes and they are then capable of recognizing each of their former acts for what it really was, divested of the illusions and mirages of their worldly life. True believers are joyous in the expectation of their

21. Imām ʿAbdallāh ibn ʿAlawī al-Ḥaddād, *The Lives of Man*, The Quilliam Press, London, 1991. Imām al-Ḥaddād (D. 1132 AH/1720 CE) was one of the most illustrious ʿAlawī scholars who was widely regarded as the 'Renewer' of the twelfth century of the Hijra.

much awaited meeting with their Lord.

This is why, as the Prophet ﷺ said, their spirits leave their bodies as smoothly as a silken robe is removed. In contrast, disbelievers dread this passage and are understandably reluctant to leave this life, the only life they are aware of. They therefore resist so much that their spirits are wrenched painfully away from their bodies, just as that same silken robe would be pulled across a bush of thorns. Between these two extremes lie all possible intermediate degrees. The Prophet's Companion, Salmān the Persian, bade his wife sprinkle perfume around his death bed, saying, 'I am visited by some of God's creation who neither eat nor drink, but are pleased with perfume.' And ʿUmar is reported to have instructed the people to repeat *Lā ilāha illa'llāh* near the dying and, if these be men of God, listen carefully to what they might utter, since, 'true things are unveiled before them.' As for Bilāl, when his wife wailed 'O Grief!' as he was dying, he replied, 'O Joy! Tomorrow I shall meet the loved ones, Muḥammad and his people.' Yet another Companion, Muʿādh ibn Jabal, was asked when dying, 'Do you see something?' and he replied, 'The spirit of my son has come to me with tidings that Muḥammad ﷺ and a hundred ranks of the Angels of Proximity and the martyrs and saints are praying for me and waiting to escort me to the Garden.'[22]

Nevertheless, death in itself is usually a painful process, as witnessed by the Prophet's death ﷺ and that of many men of God. This is why the recitation of Sūra (chapter) Yā Sīn near the dying is recommended, since it alleviates some of the pain. It is interesting to note that it is also recommended near a woman in delivery, since it eases childbirth. It is thus effective in easing one's way both into and out of this world.

'The world,' says a *ḥadīth*, 'is the believer's prison and the

22. Aḥmad, 5/243.

disbeliever's paradise.'[23] This is why, during the funeral procession, the dead, if they are believers, urge those who are carrying them to hasten, whereas the disbelievers beg them to slow down. 'The dead are aware of those who wash, carry, shroud and lower them into their graves,'[24] said the Prophet, may God's blessings and peace be upon him. They also hear the footsteps of the people walking away from them after the burial and they feel estranged.[25] Their passage to the other side is complete only after they are subjected to the sudden constriction of the grave (*qabḍat al-qabr*), and then released. Then they are visited by the two angels, Munkar and Nakīr, and interrogated about their beliefs, following which their graves become either paradisiacal or hellish until the Resurrection. 'The grave,' said the Prophet ﷺ 'is either a meadow of the meadows of the Garden, or a pit of the pits of the Fire.'[26]

It is clear from the foregoing that life in the third stage, the *barzakh* or Intermediary Realm, is far from being some kind of suspended animation as many people these days tend to think. On the contrary, it is an eventful and extremely complex existence where the consequences of one's life on earth begin to manifest themselves. It is stated unequivocally in many *ḥadīth*s that the spirits in the *barzakh* visit each other and receive each new arrival with enquiries about the affairs of their living relatives and friends.[27] The Prophet ﷺ said, 'Your deeds are shown to your dead relatives and kin, if good they rejoice, and if otherwise they say, 'O God, let them not die before You guide them as You have guided us.'[28] And once when

23. Muslim, KITĀB AL-ZUHD, 1; Tirmidhī, KITĀB AL-ZUHD, 16.

24. Aḥmad, 3/62; Ṭabarānī, *Awsaṭ*, 7/257.

25. Bukhārī, KITĀB AL-JANĀ'IZ, 68 and 87.

26. Tirmidhī, KITĀB AL-QIYĀMA, 26.

27. Ṭabarānī, *Awsaṭ*, 4/98.

28. Aḥmad, 3/164.

visiting the martyrs of Uḥud he said, 'I testify that they are alive near to God; so visit them and greet them, for by the One in whose hand my soul is, none shall greet them but that they shall greet him back, till the Day of Rising.'[29] This means that they are aware of their visitors and, when charity is given on their behalf, or some of the Qur'ān recited and offered as a gift to them, the light of these deeds reaches them in their world. This is evident from the many *ḥadīth*s encouraging people to offer the recompense for acts of worship and charity to their parents and which promise that the recompense shall be theirs, without this diminishing the givers in any way. It has also been stated in *ḥadīth* that if certain chapters of the Qur'ān, such as, al-Fātiha, al-Ikhlāṣ, and al-Takāthur are recited near the graves and the recompense for them offered to the dead, their spirits will in turn intercede for the visitor. We are advised to bury our dead among the people of virtue, for they would suffer from their evil neighbors just as the living suffer from their evil neighbors.

Some spirits are in a quasi-paradisiacal state, free to roam the universe, witness the glories of the higher worlds, meet with the Prophets and saints in ʿIllīyūn, and delight in the expectation of greater nearness to their Lord. Others, less fortunate, have their freedom curtailed to a greater or lesser extent: lesser if they are believers whose sins still require requital; and greater if they are disbelievers imprisoned in the quasi-infernal Sijjīn where their deeds recoil upon them in the form of horrifying creatures and fiery torments.

The fourth stage is that of the Resurrection, a day that for some is shorter than the batting of an eyelid, and fifty thousand years long for others. It begins with the first sounding of the Horn when all living creatures die, followed by the second sounding at which they are resurrected. All humans are then driven to the land of the gathering. The sun draws nearer so that the heat becomes so intense and

29. Ṭabarānī, *Awsaṭ*, 4/98.

the suffering so unbearable, that they begin to search for someone to intercede on their behalf so that their judgment would be speeded up, even though it may mean their being cast into the flames of Hell. Only the Prophet ﷺ will be allowed to intercede in that situation. Then all shall cross the Bridge (*Ṣirāṭ*) which is as fine as a hair, and sharper than a sword, underneath which the furnace of Hell sends its flames shooting upwards to burn and scorch those it can reach. The first to cross to safety, swifter than lightning, shall be seventy thousand believers whose faces are as radiant as the full moon. Their privilege will be to enter Paradise without having to submit to the Judgment. They shall be followed by others whose faces are as bright as the brightest stars in the night sky; they will cross as swiftly as the wind. Then others will arrive who shall cross as rapidly as birds fly, others as pure-bred horses, and others still slower, until those who shall crawl across, some of them slipping into the furnace. Those who reach the other side safely will then implore God, asking for mercy for their brothers who have fallen into the fire. They will say, 'O God! They fasted and prayed with us, and they went on pilgrimage (*ḥajj*)!' Such will be their ranks before God that He will allow them to rescue those whom they are able to recognize. Then the Scales shall be erected and the deeds weighed.

The Companions were so concerned with the perils and sufferings of that day that they prepared and planned for them by asking the Prophet ﷺ where they should seek him, in the knowledge that only his presence could guarantee safety. One of them asked the Prophet for his intercession on Judgement Day and was promised it. He then asked where he might be found and was told to try the Bridge first of all. 'What if I do not find you at the Bridge?' he asked. 'Then look for me near the Scales,' he replied. 'And if I were not to find you near the Scales?' 'Then look for me near the Pool, for I am sure to be found at one of those three places.'[30] The Pool is said to be as large as 'the distance between Sanʿā' and Madīna,'[31] and its water is 'whiter than milk and sweeter than honey.'[32] Each Prophet has a pool awaiting his nation, and the largest pool is that of the greatest Prophet and the most numerous nation. From it they will be given to drink 'a draught after which they shall never thirst again.'[33]

The fifth and most prolonged stage is that of the final abode, either of Paradise or Hell as the case may be. There the mixture of good and evil, beauty and ugliness, perfection and imperfection, and happiness and misery that characterized the previous stages is finally disentangled. Paradise shall contain all beauty, perfection and happiness, whereas Hell will be all ugliness and misery. Paradise is, by definition, the proximity of God and the higher the degree, the nearer it is to, and the brighter the unveiling will be of, the Divine Light. Hell, on the other hand, is nothing but remoteness from God; and therefore, its torments and sufferings increase the further away the degree due to the ever thickening veils between the damned and the Divine mercy.

In these dimensions every single act, thought or intention that occurred in the course of earthly life will be projected against the immeasurable screen of eternity and magnified accordingly. This is why the repercussions of words and deeds which might have seemed rather insignificant on earth appear disproportionate in the hereafter.

---

30. Tirmidhī, KITĀB AL-QIYĀMA, 9.

31. Bukhārī, KITĀB AL-RIQĀQ, 53.

32. Muslim, KITĀB FAḌĀ'IL AL-ṢAḤĀBA, 37; AḤMAD, 2/158.

33. Bukhārī, KITĀB AL-RIQĀQ, 53.

SPIRIT AND SOUL

A variety of terms are met with in Islamic writings concerning the interrelationships of the body, the soul, and the spirit. Many of these terms refer to the same realities seen from different perspectives. We thus need to define these terms and shall proceed to do so according to the school of Imām al-Ghazālī, one of the greatest-ever Islamic scholars, and by far the most authoritative writer on the subject. Ghazālī states that each of the terms—heart, spirit, soul and mind or intellect—has two meanings, a higher and a lower one. All these terms coincide in their higher meanings but differ in their lower meanings.

The heart (*al-qalb*), in its lower meaning, is the physical fleshy organ in the left side of the chest, the function of which is to distribute the blood to the various regions of the body and, along with the blood, the life energy or vital spirit. In its higher meaning it is the spiritual centre, which is the essential reality of man as a thinking and responsible being.

The spirit (*al-rūḥ*), in its lower meaning, is the vital spirit (*al-rūḥ al-ḥayawānī*), which is the energy circulating with the blood to each part of the body to where it is needed for the various faculties of the body to function. It is the same life energy that flows in animals and it has nothing specifically human about it. When it is extinguished, the body ceases to function and is said to have died. In its higher meaning, the spirit is the incorporeal reality, which coincides with the second or higher definition of the heart, and is a Divine mystery beyond the comprehension of men: *Say: The spirit is of the command of my Lord, and of knowledge you have been given but a little* (17:85).

The soul, psyche, or ego (*al-nafs*), in its lower aspect, is the term used to denote the soul which is wholly driven by the two forces of physical appetite and aggression, to the extent of ignoring or wilfully transgressing conventional moral limits. These are approximate equivalents of the concepts of pleasure seeking and pain avoidance, both of which may be either physical or mental. This is the 'soul that incites to evil' (*al-nafs al-ammāra bi'l-sū'*), which we shall label the ego, and it is to this aspect of the soul that the following famous *ḥadīth* applies, 'Your greatest enemy is your ego, that which is between your two flanks.'[34] It is this aspect that religion strongly enjoins us to subdue and control. In its higher aspect the soul is no different from the higher aspects of the heart and the spirit where they coincide. In this aspect it is termed the 'serene soul' or 'soul at peace' (*al-nafs al-muṭma'inna*). There is a transitional stage between the higher and lower aspects which is termed the 'reproachful soul' (*al-nafs al-lawwāma*), which is the soul in the process of transformation from being bestially-driven to being spiritually-driven.

The intellect (*al-ᶜaql*) in its lower aspect is the faculty which processes the information received from the sensory apparatus, organizes it, selects the relevant items and proceeds in logical steps. Thus defined it coincides with reason. In its higher aspect, the 'inspired intellect' (*al-ᶜaql al-mulham*) is the recipient of knowledge from the higher worlds. This knowledge is received directly, meaning that it does not have to enter through the senses, and is called 'inspiration.' It is not the same as the sudden flashes of insight that the ordinary mind is capable of and which differentiate it from a computer. In this higher aspect it is synonymous with the heart, the spirit and the serene soul.

To serve the heart there are a number of faculties. Firstly, there are the innate tendencies for pleasure seeking and pain avoidance. Both pleasure and pain may be mental as well as physical, immediate as well as delayed. Pleasure seeking and pain avoidance constitute the basis of motivation and volition. Secondly, there is the motor power to carry out what has been willed; this is termed capability. Thirdly,

34. ᶜAjlūnī, *Kashf al-Khafā*, 1/160, ascribed to Bayhaqī's *Kitāb al-Zuhd*.

there is the ability to perceive the environment in order to be able to influence it. This ability is both physical and psychological. The physical ability consists of the sensory system, while the psychological ability, which is located in the head, consists of five components.

Here Ghazālī is forced to depart from his strict adherence to revealed knowledge, since the faculties in question are not discussed in any detail there. Hence, in this part of his exposition, and only in this part, does he draw on the writings of the philosopher-physicians such as Ibn Sīnā, whose conception of such matters is largely, but by no means totally, based on the Greek philosophers. Thus Ghazālī mentions a faculty of 'synthetic perception' which organizes the information acquired through the senses and produces complex perceptions. He cites another faculty concerned with the perception of meaning within forms, which is able to connect sweetness with sugar, fear with wolves, and com- fort with mothers. There is a kind of memory that stores and recalls sensory information and another that stores and recalls the meanings attached to that information. Finally he mentions the imaginative and thinking faculty which processes both forms and meanings, adduces and deduces, combines and separates. When operating with forms or images this faculty is called imagination, and when operating with abstractions it is called cognition.

The heart or spirit needs these faculties in much the same manner as a traveler needs a means of locomotion and adequate supplies to enable him to reach his destination. The destination of the spirit, the real purpose for which it was created, is its meeting face to face with its Creator. It cannot reach its destination without traveling through the material world, for this is the journey that permits it to ascend the ladder of spiritual growth until the stage that qualifies it for the 'meeting.' In the material world, the body constitutes its means of locomotion and provides the various faculties necessary to enable it to gather the supplies it survives on as it travels along. The spirit therefore needs to look after the body, nourish and protect it against whatever may disturb or stop its proper functioning. The motivation to do so arises from the pleasure seeking and pain avoiding tendencies, while the means to do so comes from our physical powers and sensory system.

The spirit is neither a body, nor even a subtle substance. In its essential reality, it is immortal and unaffected by contingencies. It is not 'inside' the body, rather it is utilizing it as a craftsman utilizes a tool. However, to speak of it as 'inside' the body has always been adopted as a figure of speech to allow the expression of things which might otherwise have been too difficult to grasp. Matters concerning the spirit, as with all matters concerning the higher worlds, are always expressed symbolically and in the most practicable and profitable manner, because human language is, by its very nature, incapable of explicitly conveying spiritual truths. The vital spirit, as well as both the physical and the psychological faculties, are servants of the spirit. It breaks off its attachment to the body at death and resumes it in a different mode at the resurrection.

Man has material properties which he shares with inanimate matter; other properties, such as metabolism, growth, and reproduction, he shares with plants. He has the ability to move and interact with members of his and other species, and this he shares with animals. Some more complex forms of behavior he shares with the higher apes. What is exclusively his is the intellect in both its cognitive and spiritual levels. Thus a man becomes truly human to the extent that his heart or spirit is effectively in control, and is unimpeded by lower elements: *They have hearts but they understand not with them; they have eyes but they perceive not with them; they have ears but they hear not with them. They are like cattle; nay, they are further astray. Those are the heedless* (7:179). Understanding is here attributed to the heart, for it is with the heart and not with the mind that one may perceive the higher meanings of the signs that are within oneself and one's environment. The loss of this ability leads to seeing the form but failing to perceive its meaning; there is then no difference between this kind of perception and that of cattle. Animals are at the mercy of their pleasure seeking and pain avoiding tendencies, and they thus perceive the world in a limited, purely utilitarian, unidimensional manner. More over, humans functioning at such a low level of awareness remain at the mercy of satanic influences and are thus liable to become sub-bestial and demonic in their behavior. This is the meaning of their being further astray than cattle, and of the Qur'ānic passages where mention is made of devils of both men and jinn (6:112).

The soul is subject to the downward pull of the bestial appetites and when it surrenders to them unconditionally the result is unrestrained indulgence in eating, drinking, sleeping and mating. It is also subject to the downward pull of the lower invisible worlds, which gain a hold through its moral weaknesses and baser traits. When a man surrenders to these, he becomes a demon in human form, and such people are clearly much more injurious to themselves and others than the first kind. Both these forces, when not in total control of a person, may nevertheless result in a dissipating tendency which keeps him ever engaged in trivial activities which, although neither legally forbidden nor morally reprehensible, are a waste of precious time and energy and a diversion from concentrating on the one important thing, which is his future life.

The soul is also subject to the upward pull of the higher worlds since these are the origin of the spirit and the place it aspires to return to. This upward pull needs to overcome the other two tendencies to free itself for the ascent it yearns for.

The human soul is thus subject to three kinds of influences which can be differentiated from one another in the following way. The first, satanic insinuations (*waswās*), are recognized by their shifting character. The Devil does not really care what you are doing as long as it is either sinful or at the very least wasteful. He will thus whisper one suggestion after the other until one of them is accepted and acted upon. The Devil never enters into a rational debate, and he always evades any attempt at being cornered into a fixed position. He will swiftly change from one irrelevant argument to another, often choosing arguments which are emotionally charged and thus capable of eliciting an unrestrained response. When a person becomes angry he is more attuned to the nature of the lower worlds, for both anger and the Devil are fire, so that the angry man is much more receptive to the Devil's suggestions than the calm man. This is why the Prophet ﷺ strongly advised people not to fall prey to anger and, that should ever do so, to sit down, then lie down or, if still on fire, to have a cold bath.

The insinuations of the Devil are different from the thoughts (*khawāṭīr*) arising from the lower tendencies of the soul itself, the ego. These are characterized by their insistent quality, with the soul never being inclined to give up the pleasure it demands until fully gratified. It shows more consistency than the Devil and is amenable to some kind of logic, provided it is backed up by arguments of the same nature as itself. For example, it can be prevented from the temptation to steal by reminding it that despite the pleasure to be obtained from the money it intends to appropriate, it might very well get caught and the punishment may then be too painful to be worth the risk. Unrestrained pleasure-seeking ought, then, to be countered with the fear of punishment, either in this life or the next. This puts the pleasure-seeking tendency in open conflict with the pain-avoiding one; the latter is then supported with similar arguments of the same kind until victorious.

Second, there are the angelic inspirations (*ilhāmāt*). These encourage one to behave virtuously and are spiritually uplifting. The angelic suggestions are frequently subject to attempts of subversion or negation by the Devil. Third, there are the inspirations of Divine origin which are concerned with the love of God, longing for Him, and knowledge of the higher worlds.

Let us elucidate this schema of metapsychological influences further by restating it in slightly different terms. For the sake of convenience, we shall speak of man as made of a body, a soul and a spirit. The soul is here envisaged as the spirit in its lowest level but one, that is, the level most closely interconnected with the body and influenced by it. The vital spirit will constitute its lowest component. The soul may be spoken of as a reality in its own right and thus perceived as having two faces, one facing upwards to the spirit, the other facing downwards to the body. The soul is further thought of as being made up of two components, one cognitive and the other emotional. Each will consequently also have two faces. The upper face of the cognitive faculty will blend with the intellect in the higher sense as stated by Ghazālī, that is, the faculty capable of receiving direct Divine inspiration. The lower face will be the reasoning faculty, the imagination, and various memory stores. As for the upper face of the emotional component, it is that which experiences the love of God and the attraction of the higher worlds. At a somewhat lower level but still within the higher aspect are the emotional correlates of the virtues, such as compassion, generosity and courage. The lower face consists of the emotions in their egoistic mode on the emotional correlates of vices such as greed and conceit, and the two basic passions of physical appetites and aggression.

The behavior of a person will be conditioned by that aspect which has ascendancy over the others. When the physical appetites are given free rein, the person becomes animal-like, with his reason and his emotions both at the service of his passions. The spiritual dimension is dammed up and rendered ineffective. When emotions are given free rein they contaminate all thinking processes, becoming open to bias and prejudice. The spiritual dimension is here again neutralized. But if reason is allowed sole ascendancy, one becomes cold, calculating and machine-like. Such persons are industrially exploitable, they may be productive in research and other practical endeavors; but they remain narrow and materialistic and always open to the temptation to use any means, however inhuman, to reach their goals.

The normal state of a human being is for his physical appetites and moral weaknesses to be controlled by his aggressive tendency, which in turn should be dominated by his reason, for the real function of aggression is to be directed against evil, whether within or without oneself. Reason should be tempered, not subverted, by emotions, with both being spiritually regulated. Each of these levels is intimately related to all the others, and each reciprocally affects all the others. For instance, cognition may arouse emotions, and emotions will have physiological correlates, such as increases in the speed at which the heart beats, blood pressure, breathing, sweating, and so on, these physical reactions in turn arouse other cognitions, that arouse more emotions, and so on.

This vicious circle is broken when one learns to change his emotions by altering his thoughts, and one learns to alter his thoughts by studying the pattern of the Sunna and imitating it as much as possible. Thus a person whose soul belongs to the serene level, who has learned to detach himself from ephemeral things and commits himself to the mercy and solicitude of his Lord in the certainty that these will never fail him, will no longer be subject to the anxious thoughts and perpetual tension that contemporary man experiences as a result of his lifestyle. But a soul in a state of constant unawareness of its Lord and the life to come, whose whole energy is concentrated in its attachment to the flux of worldly things, will be in constant watchful tension, always fearing the worst, always dissatisfied with the turn of events. The more a person's consciousness is concentrated on the lower aspects of his soul and is absent from the higher ones, the more subject he will be to all kinds of suggestions and conditioning, and vice versa. The higher the focus of his consciousness, the more freedom and self-determination he possesses. Thus one is functioning ideally only when one's physiological, emotional and cognitive processes are totally regulated by that which is the very highest in man.

The brain is the junction between the psychological and the physical domains. It is the location where synthetic perception, memory, imagination and logical thinking are translated from the subtle psychological to the dense physical, and vice versa. A healthy brain is consequently necessary for normal mental functioning and any kind of pathology at any level will affect it according to its nature, location and extent. When perception, information processing, or memory are affected, behavior will also be affected. Although consciousness, in its higher sense, is not a physical phenomenon, it cannot manifest itself in the physical world nor exercise any action within it except by using the physical instrument that is the brain. In the extreme case of psychotic illness or madness, the body's dysfunction renders it useless for the spirit's purposes, and therefore the spirit's attachment to the body weakens and is reduced to the very minimum necessary to keep the body alive until such time as it either recovers or dies. The spirit's influence is, as it were, withdrawn from earthly events; and the greater the brain's dysfunction, the greater the withdrawal of the spirit. This eventually leads to the state known in the West as 'becoming a vegetable,' an expression which, crude and insensitive as it is, nevertheless indicates that what was making the body human is no longer there.

PERSONALITY

There are in each individual elements that are fixed and others that are capable of spontaneous change or deliberate modification. Together both constitute personality, that is, the pattern specific to each individual member of the human race. Outwardly observable behavior is the external manifestation of the internal interactions between these elements as well as the interpersonal social interactions between the same elements in different people.

Referring to the fixed elements, the Prophet ﷺ said, 'If you hear that a mountain has moved from its place, believe it, but if you hear that a man's character has changed, do not believe it, he remains as he was made.'[35] And he said, 'The best among you in the *Jāhiliyya* (the days of ignorance before Islam) are the best among you in Islam,'[36] meaning that those possessed of the noblest elements in their days of idolatry retain them after accepting Islam. The change from disbelief to Islam means that a cognitive restructuring must necessarily have taken place, accompanied by its emotional correlates. The fixed elements are the forces of natural appetites, temperament and intelligence. To give one example, ʿUmar ibn al-Khaṭṭāb, the second Rightly-Guided Caliph, was known to be quick-tempered and prone to violence. In his pre-Islamic days these tendencies were given free rein. Following his acceptance of Islam they remained, but were put to the service of his faith and not his ego, and kept strictly within the limits of Islamic law (*Sharīʿa*).

As for the second, changeable kind of characteristic, these are mainly the praiseworthy attributes termed virtues, such as truthfulness, fortitude, generosity and so on, and the reprehensible attributes termed vices, such as dishonesty, avarice, rancour and so

---

35. Aḥmad, 6/443.

36. Bukhārī, KITĀB AL-ANBIYĀ', 8 and 14; and Muslim, KITĀB FAFAḌĀ'IL AL-ṢAḤĀBA, 168.

on. That these attributes can be modified may be understood from the Prophet's numerous injunctions to his Companions to acquire the virtues and free themselves from vices. This means that one can train oneself to resist one's weaknesses and develop one's virtues until they become second nature. An example of this is the *ḥadīth* stating that a man may lie and carry on lying until he is confirmed as a liar before God, that is, until lying becomes second nature to him. The same also mentions the opposite case, that of the man who persists in being truthful until confirmed as one of the veracious in the presence of God.[37]

Muslim authors regard personality as a product of innate constitution modified by environmental factors. Innate constitution includes heredity, both physical and psychological, the combination of the four elements (fire, air, water and earth in their modes of hot, dry, cold and wet), and the correspondence of this combination with the signs of the zodiac and the various planets. This is a vastly complex matter, since the possible permutations are endless. The source of confusion for modern minds is that because of the current materialism they tend to take everything literally and forget that the four elements were never intended to be identified with their visible familiar counterparts, but were only called fire, air, water and earth to indicate a correspondence between them and the visible elements. These four elements are the origin of all matter, they themselves originating in a common principle, the undifferentiated Hyle (Hayūlā, i.e. primordial matter). The same applies to the correspondence of the seven heavens with the seven planets. Each heaven is designated by the name of the planet that corresponds to it most closely, but the heavens can by no means be identified with the orbits of these planets since the planets are in the visible sky whereas the heavens are in the invisible subtle domain.

37. Bukhārī, KITĀB AL-ADAB, 69.

These terms are taken literally only if the correspondence between the different degrees or dimensions of existence is lost sight of. These correspondences and their implications for medicine, psychology, sociology, history, and other sciences were understood by many of the civilizations preceding Islam and are not specifically Islamic. They were perceived by the Muslims, whether religious scholars, philosophers or Sufis, as possessing a basis in truth and were adopted with minor variations between different schools. Such a perspective, however, has become so alien to today's mentality and so unlikely to be put to practical use that we shall not pursue its discussion further. Because of the importance of heredity, there is in *ḥadīth* specific advice on how to choose a wife, stressing the need to avoid choosing a woman from a vile background simply because of her beauty. There are also criteria for fathers to assess their prospective sons-in-law.

As for environmental factors, they begin soon after birth with the *adhān*, the call to the ritual prayer, in the right ear of each newborn and the *iqāma*, the second call heralding the actual beginning of the prayer, in his left. Mothers are enjoined to breastfeed their infants for about two years. Milk is considered the vehicle of important influences, and this is why marriage between those who have had a common wet-nurse is prohibited. The importance of the kind and amount of food the child is given as he grows is stressed. Food must be *ḥalāl*, from legally permissible sources and, more often than not, frugal. The child must be taught, albeit not too early, that Muslims must be people 'who eat only when hungry, and when they eat they stop short of satiety.' And, 'Never does the Son of Adam fill a vessel worse than his stomach. It is enough for the Son of Adam to have a few morsels to keep his back straight. But if he must, then let him assign one third to his food, one third to his beverage, and one third to his breath.'[38]

Then comes the education the child receives, the ideas and values

38. Tirmidhī, KITĀB AL-ZUHD, 42; Ibn Māja, KITĀB AL-AṬʿIMA, 50.

which are inculcated in him, the style of thinking he is trained to adopt, and the people he is allowed to mix with. Children learn their habits from the environment. This is how they learn their social manners, how to behave with each member of the community according to his status, how to eat, drink, sleep, jest, pray, fast, and so on. As children grow older, their intelligence develops according to the pattern of their parents and teachers, and they are taught the beliefs and assumptions which their people live by. Finally, there are each person's own wishes and ambitions, which drive him to develop this or that character.

The personality of a human being is vastly complex, and all attempts at fitting people into neat pigeon holes must necessarily flounder. There are many different systems of reference which may be used to characterise a person, each system having a specific purpose as well as possessing limitations. It is possible to classify people according to their spiritual level, as described earlier, as those with an 'Inciting Soul' or ego, those with a 'Reproachful Soul,' and those with a 'Serene Soul.' Smaller subdivisions along the same scale have also been expounded.

A similar form of characterisation is to classify the person as a type according to which of the faculties of physical appetites, aggression, emotional nobility, intellect, or spirituality are dominant. Imām Abū'l-ʿAzā'im[39] describes four types according to this framework. There are those who resemble cattle or whose egos are dominant: when their desire for physical pleasure is aroused they hasten to gratify it and are unconcerned if in the process they create a scandal or bring shame upon themselves and their families. There are those who resemble predators or whose pride and irascible element

39. Imām Muḥammad Mādi Abū'l-ʿAzā'im (D.1365 AH/1937 CE), a teacher at Khartoum University, was one of the most important Egyptian scholars and spiritual masters of the last century.

are dominant: they will endure poverty and hunger and feel too proud to ask anyone for help, and are prepared to endure hardships to achieve social prominence and political power. They control their appetites for the sake of their reputation. There are also those in whom the lower aspect of the intellect, that is the rational faculty, is dominant and coupled with nobility, which in this context is taken to mean their power to control appetites, aggression and lower drives. They cannot endure shame or dishonour and need to preserve their self-respect. Their type is intermediate between the predatory and the angelic. Finally there are those who resemble angels in that the higher aspect of the intellect is supreme in them: they love, hate and act solely for the sake of their Lord.

Temperament as resulting from the four humours that correspond to the four elements is another manner of characterization.

The virtues and vices as described in treatises of ethics may also be used to type personality, and the position of each person can be measured on a number of axes, each having a virtue at one pole and its opposing vice on the other. To the presence or absence of each virtue and its measure, may be added the cognitive correlates. The cognitive structure of each individual may thus be charted as well as other matters of particular individual importance added to complete the picture: *Each behaves according to his kind* (17:84). The word 'kind' is taken here to refer to religion, knowledge, temperament, virtues, vices, or emotional constitution. Ultimately, however, it must be taken back all the way to the person's archetype that subsists in the immutable Divine knowledge.

DREAMS

Released by sleep from having to attend to the physical world, the spirit turns its attention to the invisible dimensions. It may roam the Intermediary Realm with all its degrees, ascend to the spiritual world, or even soar up to the Divine Throne and beyond it to the Divine Presence. These are dream-visions (*ru'yā*). The spirit may also have visions of people and events in a manner similar to that of the World of Similitudes, which is equivalent to the imagination at the individual level. This means that what is seen is only an image, not an actually witnessed event, yet it is nonetheless true. This is one kind of dream. There are two other kinds, those arising from the soul or psyche and those arising from the lower subtle domain, for dreams are subject to the same kinds of influences that we discussed earlier in the context of the tendencies of the soul and the origin of thoughts.

The first kind, the dream-vision, is of either angelic or Divine origin. It is crystal clear, has a compelling quality about it, may have one or more meanings, and frequently involves meetings with Prophets, angels, men of God, departed relatives or friends, and journeys to holy places such as Makka, Madīna, or any other place of spiritual importance. To this category also belong premonitory dreams, which may be due to the spirit witnessing an event in the higher worlds before it comes to pass in the physical realm, or to someone informing him of it. The Prophet ﷺ said, 'Those who see me will have seen me in truth, for the Devil cannot impersonate me.'[40] This means that no lower influence can masquerade as the Prophet, and this is understood to apply to all other Prophets and men of God. It is also known that the dead, being in the abode of truth, usually utter the truth in dreams. The meaning of dream-visions is sometimes evident at first sight, but sometimes needs to be interpreted. The dreamer usually awakens feeling serene and sometimes joyous and delighted with what he has seen.

---

40. Bukhārī, KITĀB AL-ʿILM, 38; and KITĀB AL-TAʿBĪR, 10; Muslim, KITĀB AL-RU'YĀ, 10 and 11.

The second kind of dream is the ordinary dream that originates in the soul and concerns mundane things and persons of no great consequence. The dream is produced by the movements of the soul, its hopes, worries, sorrows and emotions such as love, jealousy and anger, the events of the day or the preceding days, wishful thinking, and sometimes by physical factors such as cold, heat, indigestion, hunger and thirst.

The third kind is the demonic dream, which is more or less nightmarish, contains lurid or frightening images, and is generally a chaotic experience which leaves one feeling fear, foreboding or disgust.

The classification of dreams into dream-visions, ordinary dreams and demonic dreams is necessary because each kind is dealt with differently. Dream-visions are Divine gifts that gladden the heart and bring good tidings. They should neither be interpreted lightly nor by people who lack expertise. They should not even be indiscriminately divulged to anyone, except those who are both discreet and qualified to understand them. They are neither a matter for speculation nor open discussion. Ordinary dreams, on the other hand, may simply be ignored; they carry no great weight for ill or good. As for demonic dreams, the instruction in the various *ḥadīth*s regarding them is to ask God swiftly for protection against whatever evil may be in them, and having remembered God and thus entered into His fortress one should turn onto one's other side, go back to sleep, and refrain from mentioning the dream to anyone. When this is done, say the *ḥadīth*s, no harm shall come of such dreams.

However, in reality things are much more complex than the simple impression this schematic representation may give. Dream-visions may be either contaminated by psychic or demonic elements, which may obfuscate the meaning and mislead the dreamer as to the true nature of the experience. Dreams lose their clarity when the fissures between us and the lower worlds widen and so their influence is felt more pervasively. This is why Muslims are always encouraged to close all possible fissures which might allow the irruption of influences from the lower dimensions and to open all possible gates into the higher dimensions in order to counteract these influences. Thus the demonic dream should be counteracted by the remembrance of God and the instruction not to dwell on it or mention it, but rather to forget it and trust in God's protection. This is the exact opposite of what is done in psychoanalysis, and we shall return to this point later. Premonitory dreams may also arouse feelings of fear and foreboding, although when interpreted correctly much of what usually arouses people's fears turns out to be totally innocuous. There are also dreams that are triggered off by demonic suggestions which arouse certain lustful elements in the soul and then leave it to carry out the rest of the experience by itself. As with daydreaming, the experience may be much less chaotic than a full-blown nightmare.

What is currently known in the West about the physiology of sleep amounts to no more than the reaction of the brain to the events in the subtle domains that we have discussed.[41] The brain is the organ used by the spirit to carry out the various functions outlined earlier, and not, as is thought in the West, the main instigator of these functions.

As for the interpretation of dreams, it is an ancient science which depends on the understanding of symbolism. The most authoritative interpreter of dreams in Islam was Ibn Sīrīn[42] who was one of the Followers (*Tābi'ūn*), or those born in the first generation after the Prophet, may God's peace be upon him. According to Ibn Sīrīn, the veracity of the dream depends on the goodness of the dreamer,

41. Muslim jurists have divided sleep for their purposes into heavy and light, long and short, and have detailed the legal rulings concerning each kind.

42. Ibn Sīrīn (D.110 AH/728-29 CE) was the foremost authority on dream interpretation as well as an authoritative all-round scholar. His book on the interpretation of dreams remains the basic text on the subject to this day.

since the *ḥadīth* states that, 'Those whose dream visions are the truest are those who are the most veracious in speech.'[43] That even disbelievers such as Pharaoh and Nebuchadnezzar sometimes saw veracious dreams is explained by the fact that these dreams were of import to someone else, Joseph in the first case, and Daniel in the second, both of whom were Divine Prophets. The dream interpreter, says Ibn Sīrīn, should have proficient knowledge of the Qur'ān and *ḥadīth* their language, manners of expression, symbols and allegories, as well as the sayings of the ancient Prophets and sages, poetry, proverbs, semantics and the derivation of words. He should eat lawful food, behave with rectitude and sincerity, and be truthful in speech. He should pay attention to the core of the dream and not be sidetracked by elements which may be psychic or demonic. As each dream may have one or more good sides to it and one or more evil sides, the emphasis should be laid on those features which are consonant with the general state of the dreamer, his life history and current behavior.

To show how dreams are deciphered by such interpreters let us take a few examples from Ibn Sīrīn's book. Apart from higher beings, Prophets, men of God and angels who obviously never lie, other beings whose speech is generally accepted as true are children and animals, as both are innocent. In contrast, those whose speech is expected to be un-true in the waking state are also expected to lie with regards to dreams. This concerns such people as astrologers, soothsayers and their like. Things which change with the seasons, such as trees, fruits, clothes and so on, are interpreted as referring to the nature of that season. Other things are interpreted according to their genus, then their species, and then their special attributes. For example, trees, beasts, and birds are interpreted by their genus to be people. So if the species of the tree is the palm tree, the man is an Arab

43. Tirmidhī, KITĀB AL-RU'YĀ, I.

since palm trees are most common in the land of the Arabs. If the species of the bird is a peacock, the man is a non-Arab. If the bird is a predator, such as the eagle for instance, this attribute is interpreted as belonging to a king; a crow de-notes someone who is treacherous or a liar. There are also other symbolic interpretations for each of the things that we have mentioned. Sometimes the thing is interpreted as its opposite. For instance, weeping may be interpreted as the approach of relief from suffering, laughter to mean sorrow, the winner in a wrestling bout to be the loser in real life and so on.

Ibn Sīrīn cites the dreams of the Companions as an example of how the differences between dreamers leads to great differences of interpretation. As they were attached to the next world, their dreams were interpreted accordingly: when they saw dates they interpreted them as the sweetness of their religion, and honey represented the recitation of the Qur'ān. But for people attached to worldly things, dates and honey will almost always signify physical pleasures. There are no systematic expositions of the technique of interpretation. Extant books on the subject do no more than list the interpretations most likely to be given to each image or kind of images with warnings about rash interpretations. Even Ibn Sīrīn was said to have spent half a day interrogating a dreamer about the details of his inward and outward life before venturing to interpret his dream. He was said by his disciples to have interpreted no more than one dream out of every forty that were recounted to him. Most men of God are reluctant to interpret dreams and discourage other people from doing so. As far as Muslim psychotherapists are concerned, the interpretation of dreams is in no way an indispensable or even very important part of therapy. We do not need to study the subject or become experts, it being more than enough to know the general rules and to be guided accordingly by them.

It may be appropriate however, to say a few words hereabout

symbols in general, for an understanding of the principle of symbolism is beneficial not only in understanding dreams, but in seeing through the pseudo interpretation of the analysts, and in understanding much that the literal-minded mentality of today has put out of reach. A symbol is a concrete image used to indicate something that is invisible and imperceptible through the sensory apparatus. It is the means of conveying at a stroke meanings that are either too subtle to be explained in plain words or too high to be expressed unveiled.

Symbols are used with great frequency in the Qur'ān, *ḥadīth*, poetry and spiritual writings. Each symbol must share an essential attribute with the thing it is used to indicate. For instance, the heart, being the centre of one's physical being, is used to indicate the centre of a place, an organization, or of one's consciousness. In the first two cases the thing indicated is at the same level of existence as the symbol, namely the physical realm. Symbolism proper, however, uses an image from one level to indicate a reality from a higher level. To return to the image of the heart, when used to indicate the centre of the soul it is already pointing at a higher level, namely the invisible psychic level. This is how expressions such as 'heavy-hearted' and 'light-hearted' came to be used and understood immediately. At a higher level still the term 'heart' is used to indicate the spirit in its highest aspect and this is why it is said that, 'The heart of the believer is the Throne of the All-Merciful.' The Kaᶜba is the spiritual heart of the terrestrial world, and it is also the projection on the material plane of all the Houses in the higher heavens up to the Populous House, which is the heart of the universe. The *Kaᶜba* therefore corresponds outwardly to what the heart is inwardly, and this is why we term the *Kaᶜba* the 'heart of the world,' and the Populous House the 'heart of the universe.' Thus the Qur'ānic verse, *Purify My House for those who circle around it, retreat in it, bow and prostrate* (22:26), is taken by Imām al-Ḥaddād to refer to the heart with the various influences from the surrounding dimensions revolving around it. Similarly, the physical heart which sends blood and warmth throughout the body is a symbol of the heart of the man of God which radiates lights. The Kaᶜba, which radiates the blessings it receives from the higher world throughout the terrestrial world, and the Populous House, which radiates light throughout the universe, are also symbolised by the heart. These correspondences are based on the fact that each dimension, as we said before, is the shadow cast by the dimension immediately above it. Hence there could not have been people circumambulating the earthly Kaᶜba had not this model existed in the higher worlds, namely the angels and spirits circling around the Populous House and higher still, around the Divine Throne.

An image from the world of forms is therefore capable of pointing to a higher reality from the subtle domain, to a higher level in the spiritual world where meanings are formless, or even higher to that reality's archetype in Divine knowledge which resolves in combinations of Divine Names and Attributes, and beyond that the indescribable Divine Essence. Therefore, the verse stating that, *To God belongs the highest similitude* (16:60), may be taken to mean that the highest meaning of any symbol is God Himself. This is why the traditional commentaries say that the 'highest similitude' is *Lā ilāha illa'llāh*.

Another example from *ḥadīth* is the following, 'You have returned the best of returns, you have returned from the smaller struggle to the greater struggle, the struggle of a servant against his passions.'[44] The image of men-at-arms battling against each other is used here to render intelligible the battle between the lower bestial and demonic aspects of the human being and his higher spiritual

44. Bayhaqī, KITĀB AL-ZUHD, 2/165.

tendencies. That this inner battle is more essential and real than the outer one is made clear by its being termed the 'greater' *Jihād*. Both kinds of *Jihād* are smaller versions of the cosmic battle between good and evil, where the forces of evil are personified by Satan and his host and the forces of good by the Supreme Assembly and their representatives at each level of existence.

As a final example let us mention the frequent comparison of the Prophet with the full moon. The light of the sun is too powerful to be looked at directly, but one can look at its reaction from the surface of the moon. Similarly, the Divine Light cannot be gazed at, but its reflection in the Prophet ﷺ can be. Here, the correspondence between the symbols and what they represent is quite easy to see.

The universal pattern is that, as one ascends through the various levels, organization, harmony, beauty and perfection increase, and the closer one approaches the absolute perfection of God, the greater these principles become. Likewise, the farther one descends in the opposite direction, the more chaotic and evil things become. Thus, the collective unconscious where Carl Jung searches for his pseudo-archetypes is in fact nothing but the demonic and chaotic lower world.

3. THE TIMES

Revelation teaches us that mankind is set on an inexorable course of deterioration which is to end only by the advent of the Hour. Since Islam is the pillar and *raison d'etre* of the civilization that flourishes on its land, the degree of decay of that civilization is to be measured primarily by the degree to which religion itself has weakened. The criteria according to which such an assessment should be made were given in great detail by the Prophet ﷺ to his Companions over the years, and were summed up in a long speech he made during the course of the Farewell Pilgrimage, when he stood weeping before the door of the Kaʿba holding its handle, and then proceeded to entrust his Companions with the knowledge of what was to come: a trust they were to transmit to succeeding generations so that one day it would reach us and enable us to guard ourselves against the coming perils.

The first three generations of Muslims were proclaimed by the Prophet ﷺ to be superior to all those who were to follow them. This is despite the fact that those to follow were more 'civilized,' the essential criterion here being nearness to God and profound understanding of religion rather than material welfare.

He said ﷺ 'The best among my nation are the generation among whom I was raised, then the one that follows, then the one that follows that;[45] and, 'The upright will depart one after another and there will remain refuse like that of barley or dates;[46] and, 'The knots of Islam will be undone one after the other. Whenever a knot is undone the people will hold on tightly to the next. The first to become undone is judgement (according to the Law) and the last the ritual prayer';[47] and, 'Islam began as a stranger and will revert to being a stranger as it once was. Therefore, blessed are the strangers who remain virtuous when everyone else be comes corrupt.'[48]

According to the Prophet ﷺ life is preferable to death when the times are good, but the virtuous will wish for death when the times become corrupt. 'When your rulers are of the best among you, your rich are liberal and your affairs decided by consultation among you, then the face of the earth is better for you than its belly. But when your rulers become the worst among you, your rich become miserly and your affairs are decided by your women, then the belly of the earth is better for you than its surface.'[49]

It is easy to deduce from the numerous *ḥadīth*s describing the times at the approach of the Hour that the Prophet ﷺ foresaw a progressive shift from order to chaos involving all possible parameters. This trend toward increasing deviancy will involve religious, political, social, physical, psychological and ecological parameters.

The deterioration of government is described in the following *ḥadīth*s: 'There will be after me successors (*khulafā'*), then after the successors, chiefs; then after the chiefs, kings; then after the kings,

45. Bukhārī, KITĀB FAḌĀ'IL AL-NABĪ, 1; Muslim, KITĀB FAḌĀ'IL AL-ṢAḤĀBA, 210.

46. Bukhārī, KITĀB AL-RIQĀQ, 9, and KITĀB AL-MAGHĀZĪ, 35.

47. Aḥmad, 5/251 and 4/332.

48. Muslim, KITĀB AL-IMĀN, 232; Tirmidhī, KITĀB AL-IMĀN, 3.

49. Tirmidhī, KITĀB AL-FITAN, 78.

tyrants...';[50] and, 'There will be rulers who will make your hearts warm and your skins soft, then there will be rulers who will cause your hearts to shrink back and your skins to shudder with disgust.'[51]

The successors mentioned are the Rightly-Guided Caliphs, who ruled directly after the Prophet's death, those whose following in the footsteps of their master ﷺ made them worthy of the title *khalīfa*. By 'chiefs' are meant those rulers who were first among equals, not absolute rulers, but no longer worthy of the title *khalīfa* because of their deviation from strict adherence to *Sharīʿa*, despite their continuing to use the title *khalīfa*.

By 'kings' and 'tyrants' two further degrees of remoteness from *Sharīʿa* are indicated. In kings a certain worldly nobility continues to exist, but not in tyrants who will have lost all moral restraint. Those men will be surrounded by courtiers out to further their own personal aims at the expense of the people. Many *ḥadīth*s explain this further. 'God never raised a Prophet nor established a *khalīfa* but that they were surrounded by two kinds of people, those who enjoin good and urge them to it and those who enjoin evil and urge them to it...'[52] 'No nation ever fell into dissent after its Prophet but that those who upheld falsehood vanquished those who upheld the truth.'[53] 'The best of your leaders are those whom you love and who love you, for whom you pray and who pray for you, and the worst of your leaders are those whom you hate and who hate you, whom you curse and who curse you.' They said, 'O Messenger of God, shall we fight them then?' He replied, 'Not as long as they maintain the performance of the ritual prayer among you. He who is governed by someone who commits sins let him detest the sins he

50. Ṭabarānī, *Kabīr*, 22/374; al-Haytamī, *Majmaʿ al-Zawā'id*, 5/190.

51. Aḥmad, 3/28; Bayhaqī, *Shuʿab al-Imān*, 6/64.

52. Bukhārī, KITĀB AL-QADAR, 8, and KITĀB AL-AḤKĀM, 42.

53. Tirmidhī, KITĀB AL-ZUHD, 34; Aḥmad, 3/39.

commits but not abandon obedience.'[54] 'There will come upon the people a time when the rulers will be foolish; they will advance the worst of people while pretending to raise their best and they will delay the ritual prayers from their prescribed times. Those who live through these times should refuse to act for them as aids, policemen, tax collectors or treasurers.'[55] 'There will come at the end of time iniquitous rulers, corrupt ministers, judges who betray [their trust], and scholars who lie. Those who live through their time should not act for them as aids, tax collectors, treasurers or policemen.'[56]

Such are the rulers who 'make one's heart shrink and one's skin shudder in disgust.'[57] How familiar are these feelings to today's Muslims, whose rulers have totally forgotten what *Sharᶜia* is, and how the feeling increases in those countries whose rulers still pretend to uphold *Sharīᶜa*!

The Prophet Muḥammad said, may blessings and peace be upon him, 'That which destroyed those who were before you is that when the noble among them stole they were pardoned, but when the weak among them stole they were chastised...'[58] He urged Muslims to stand firm in their adherence to *Sharīᶜa* when their rulers abandon it. 'The wheel of Islam is now in motion. Follow the Book [of God] wherever it leads you. The Book and the rulers ill separate, [so] do not abandon the Book.'[59] And he warned of the consequences of abandoning the Book: 'Their rulers will not break their pledge to God and His Messenger, but that He will send their enemies against them so that they may wrest away from them some of their riches.

54. Tirmidhī, KITĀB AL-FITAN, 77; Aḥmad, 6/34 and 38.

55. Ibn Ḥibbān, *Ṣaḥīḥ*, 10/446.

56. Ṭabaranī, *Awsaṭ*, 4/277, and *Ṣaghīr*, 1/340.

57. Muslim, KITĀB AL-IMRA'A, 65; Tirmidhī, KITĀB AL-TAFSĪR, Sura 49.

58. Bukhārī, KITĀB AL-ḤUDŪD, 13; Muslim, KITĀB AL-ḤUDŪD, 8.

59. Al-Haytamī, *Majmaᶜ al-Zawā'id*, 5/238.

They will not abandon judging by the Book of God and the Sunna of the Messenger of God, but that God will cause them to pit their might against each other.'[60]

The two barriers which stood between the Muslims and subversion were the religious and political powers, the latter's function being to protect the first and allow it to exercise its function to the full. Religious scholars are the custodians of revealed knowledge. 'Scholars are heirs to the Prophets: for Prophets bequeath neither dinar nor dirham, but they bequeath knowledge, and those who receive it will have received an ample share.'[61] The gradual disappearance of knowledge and the supremacy of ignorance will result from diminution in the number of true scholars and the increase in the number of false ones. 'God does not remove knowledge by wresting it away from the people, but He removes knowledge by taking away scholars until, when no [true] scholar remains, the people will make leaders out of ignorant men who will answer without knowledge when asked, [and] they will thereby stray and lead others astray.'[62]

The phenomenon is clearly discernible today. Whenever we hear of the departure of a great man of God and inquire about his successor we are almost always sure to find none. As for false scholars, the Prophet spoke thus to his Companions about them:

> It is a sign of the approach of the Hour that the preachers [those who do not practice what they preach] on your pulpits will abound, your scholars will consort with your rulers, they will make *ḥalāl* (lawful) for them what is *ḥarām* (unlawful) and *ḥarām* what is *ḥalāl*. They will give them the rulings they desire....[63]

You live at a time when the knowledgeable abound while the

---

60. Al-Ḥakim, *al-Mustadrak*, 4/540; al-Bayhaqī, *Shuʿab al-Imān*, 3/197; Haytamī, *Majmaʿ al-Zawā'id*, 3/65.

61. Bukhārī, KITĀB AL-ʿILM, 10.

62. Bukhārī, KITĀB AL-ʿILM, 34, and KITĀB AL-FITAN, 25; Muslim, KITĀB AL-ʿILM, 11.

63. Imām Mālik, *al-Muwaṭṭa'*, KITĀB AL-SAFAR, 88.

> preachers are few; those of you who abandon a tenth of what they have learned will go astray. There will come a time upon the people when the knowledgeable will be few while the preachers will abound; at that time, those who uphold a tenth of what they know will be saved.[64]

As for the gradually increasing distance between the common Muslims and the true practice of their religion, it was described thus.

> To everything a flow and an ebb. The flow of this religion is when the whole tribe is so knowledgeable that only a man or two keep away [from religion]. The ebb of this religion is when the whole tribe becomes distant so that only one or two knowledgeable men are found; they will be overwhelmed, humiliated and unable to find helpers or supporters.[65]

The result of this distance is the loss of moral behaviour, the disruption of kinship bonds and the inversion of normal priorities. People will become materialistic, engaged in the gratification of their bestial appetites, and ready to do anything for quick gain. They will forget that there is a life to come and that they will be held to account for every single act they do. Muslims whose conscience is alive will be affected adversely by the prevailing climate, even when they themselves are uninvolved in any wrongdoing. For example, 'There shall come a time upon the people when they will take usury, those who do not take it will be affected by the dust of it.'[66] As for those who appease their conscience with false justifications, these will abound.

'There shall come to the people years of deception, the liar shall be believed while the truthful one shall be given the lie, the treacherous one shall be trusted, while the honest one shall be mistrusted, and the *ruwaybida* shall speak. "What are the *ruwaybida*?' they

---

64. Aḥmad, 5/155; al-Haytamī, *Majmaʿ al-Zawā'id*, 1/187.

65. ʿAjlūnī, *Kashf al-Khafa*, 2/172, ascribed to Abū Nuʿaym and Ibn al-Sunnī.

66. Ibn Māja, KITĀB AL-TIJĀRA, 58; Nasā'ī, KITĀB AL-BUYŪʿ, 2.

asked, and he replied, 'Mean men discoursing on public matters.'[67] The word ruwaybida is unfamiliar, even to Arabs, but very revealing when one reflects on its meaning. Its root, r-b-d means to 'be' low,' or 'lie low,' or 'crouch.' *Ruwaybida* is the plural of the diminutive form of the word. It thus indicates not only those who are base and mean, but who are so in a weak and insignificant manner, and who are therefore failures even in being bad. One only has to take a quick look at the media to see *ruwaybida* everywhere. Ignorant people full of themselves, pronouncing on the public affairs of the Muslims, unhesitatingly giving confident opinions on matters they know next to nothing about, deceiving the people with their assurance, and leading others astray. This is yet another instance where the Prophet ﷺ spoke about things which could not possibly have been understood in the days before the mass media. Not too many years ago every Muslim community knew who was allowed to speak and who should be listening, who had knowledge and who was in need of it. No base ignorant man, no sower of discord, no scandalmonger was allowed to speak in public. Nowadays, under the pretext of freedom of speech, newspapers and TV stations compete with each other in spreading scandal, the most scandalous being sure to capture the largest audience. This is one of the most characteristic signs of the times. Other signs, as mentioned in *ḥadīth*s, are:

> There will come a time upon people when a man will not care how he gains his money, lawfully or unlawfully.[68]

> ...Rulers will come after me who neither follow my guidance nor emulate my example, those who will approve of their lies and assist them in their injustice: they are not of me, neither am I of them. They shall not come to my Pool to drink. But those who will neither confirm their lies nor assist them in their injustice: they are of me

---

67. Ibn Māja, KITĀB AL-FITAN, 24.

68. Nasā'ī, KITĀB AL-BUYŪʿ, 3 and 5.

and I of them. They shall come to my Pool to drink...[69]

There will appear at the end of time men who will sell the Hereafter for this world, they will wear eeces of sheep, so smooth they will be, their tongues will be sweeter than sugar, but their hearts will be hearts of wolves.[70]

Never do the works of a people become evil without their decorating their mosques.[71]

The dinar and the dirham have destroyed those who were before you and they will destroy you.[72]

... A man will obey his wife while antagonising his mother and draw his friend nearer while pushing his father away. There will be loud voices in the mosques. Tribes will be ruled by the most corrupt and the leader of the people shall be the vilest among them. Some people will be treated respectfully solely for fear of their evil....[73]

It is a sign of the Hour that knowledge shall disappear and ignorance predominate, that adultery and alcohol drinking shall abound.[74]

It is a sign of the nearness of the Hour that evil people will be elevated while good people will be abased, that talking will be profuse, while doing will be scarce, that writings will be read before the people that none will reprove. 'What are these writings?' it was asked. He replied, 'What was written that is other than the Book of God, August and Majestic is He.'[75]

One of the best words to describe the dominant state of today's people is egocentricity. Once everything is discarded that may have helped them to understand the purpose of their existence and their role as human beings, the centre of their consciousness ceases

69. Al-Ḥakim, *al-Mustadrak*, 4/422.

70. Tirmidhī, KITĀB AL-ZUHD, 59.

71. Ibn Māja, KITĀB AL-MASĀJID, 2.

72. Ibn Ḥibbān, *Ṣaḥīḥ*, 2/469; Ibn Abī Shayba, *Musannaf*, 7/506.

73. Tirmidhī, KITĀB AL-FITNA, 38.

74. Bukhārī, KITĀB AL-ʿILM, 21, and KITĀB AL-ḤUDŪD, 20; Muslim, KITĀB AL-ʿILM, 8 and 9.

75. Al-Ḥakim, *al-Mustadrak*, 4/554.

to be their hearts and becomes their egos. They thus become shallow, worthless and conceited people who are totally engrossed in the bestial aspects of their lives. The centre of their being becomes their ego, the lowest aspect of the soul. Such people as these are effectively worshipping their money and their bestial appetites. This is the hidden idolatry mentioned in other *ḥadīth*s. The consequence of such egocentricity is that, in their breathless venal pursuits, they shall have need to discard the religious and moral restraints of old and to justify lying, deceit and disloyalty on grounds of expediency.

Since it is a Divine rule that people are mostly governed by the rulers they deserve, their being, in a certain manner, mirror images of their societies, the people we have just described, being the worst, shall be governed by the worst. The political leadership of the Muslims was originally understood to be the prerogative of the best men in the community, or those who combined the mastery of the religious sciences with a noble, generous, stable, detached personality, and were possessed of the virtues, wisdom and force of decision that are the vital prerequisites for the adequate fulfilment of the role of *khalīfa*. Those qualities were only possessed in full by the first four Rightly-Guided Caliphs, after whom they became the exception rather than the rule, until nowadays they have disappeared entirely. However, despite the fact that, subsequent to the first four Caliphs, rulers along with their surrounding cliques have always been more or less corrupt, this corruption was largely confined to their personal behaviour and they were frequently subject to the censure and criticism of the *ʿulamā'* (scholars of religion). Such was the power of religion that the rulers, more often than not, were constrained to take heed. Thus it was that the corruption of the ruling minority did not spread to infect the whole community, which continued to live according to a hierarchy of values that never ascribed more importance to this world than the next.

As the Hour approaches, however, the most venal elements in the community will find themselves holding financial and political power. 'The most corrupt man shall lead each tribe and the vilest man shall lead each people,'[76] said the Prophet, blessings and peace be on him. He also said that we shall see, 'rapacity reigning, passions obeyed, this world given priority, and the admiration of each man for his own opinions,'[77] and 'trustworthiness is lost an responsibilities assigned to those unworthy of them.[78] 'The minds of the people of that time will be taken away: there will remain only people resembling dust, most of whom will know nothing but think they know it all.[79] Then we shall have rulers who are brutal and oppressive to their own subjects but weak and ineffectual in the face of foreign interference or coercion. They will try to consolidate their rule by silencing all criticism and will thus need to buy or corrupt the *ʿulamāʾ* to use them to further their own plans. Those who cannot be bought will be intimidated and prevented from airing their views, whether in the mosques or in the media. Some will be persecuted, imprisoned, tortured or executed. Having lost its spokesmen, the nation's vulnerability to subversion will multiply manifold. Foreign legal systems will be adopted and the rulings of *Sharīʿa* ignored. Bribes will be redefined as gifts or commissions, usury will be legalized and imposed upon everyone to the extent that it will become nearly impossible to earn a purely *ḥalāl* livelihood, since all money will be processed through the banks and will therefore be soiled even for those who do not accept interest.

One of the results of the corruption of the government and

76. Tirmidhī, KITĀB AL-FITNA, 38.

77. Tirmidhī, KITĀB AL-TAFSĪR, Sura 5; Abū Dāwūd, KITĀB AL-MALĀHIM, 4/123; Ibn Māja, KITĀB AL-FITAN, 21.

78. Bukhārī, KITĀB AL-ʿILM, 3, and KITĀB AL-RIQĀQ, 35.

79. Ibn Māja, KITĀB AL-FITAN, 10.

scholars is that, as stated in *ḥadīth* the majority of ignorant Muslims will indiscriminately adopt the ways of the West.

The Prophet ﷺ said, 'You shall follow the ways of those who were before you, handspan by handspan and cubit by cubit, to the extent that were they to enter a lizard's hole you would follow them.'[80] They asked, 'O Messenger of God! The Jews and the Christians?' He answered, 'And who else?'[81] And he said, 'The worst among this nation will follow the ways of those nations that have preceded them...' And, 'O God! Preserve me from being overtaken by a time when the knowledgeable ones will not be listened to, and the decent ones will be ignored. Their hearts shall be hearts of foreigners, while their tongues will [still] be those of Arabs.'[82] That this was fraught with peril was clearly indicated by such warnings as the following, 'He is not one of us who imitates other than us. Do not imitate the Jews and the Christians...'[83] And 'He who imitates certain people is one of them.'[84]

One of the signs of the estrangement of the nation from the Sunna of its Prophet is their abandonment of their traditional ways of dressing. The abandonment of the turban for instance was said to be a sign that Muslims will suffer humiliation and lose their dignity. 'Turbans are the crowns of the Arabs, when they put them down they shall have put down their dignity.'[85] He also said that men will again wear crowns. To say that men will wear crowns is to say that they will adopt the dress of the non-believers, since in the early days

---

80. Bukhārī, KITĀB AL-IʿTIṢAM, 14, and KITĀB AL-ANBIYĀ', 50; Muslim, KITĀB AL-ʿILM, 6.
81. Aḥmad, 4/125.
82. Ibid., 5/340.
83. Tirmidhī, KITĀB AL-ISTI'DHĀN, 7, and KITĀB AL-ADAB, 41.
84. Abū Dāwūd, KITĀB AL-LIBĀS, 4.
85. Bayhaqī, *Shuʿab al-Imān*, 5/176.

of Islam the Muslims saw the Persians wearing headdresses which at the time were described as looking like crowns. Today it may be taken to refer to western-style hats or helmets. The meaning of this portion of the *ḥadīth* is that people will abandon their dignified and traditional way of dressing, including their turbans. The importance of the turban has always been obvious to Muslims and it has therefore been worn by every male Muslim throughout the nation from Morocco to Malaysia and from Mauritania to Turkestan uninterruptedly for fourteen centuries. Only recently have people begun to forget that, for Muslims, courtesy in the mosque and in social gatherings means keeping one's head covered, preferably with a turban, as opposed to other people's habit of removing their hats as an expression of courtesy.

The prohibition against men wearing women's clothes and vice versa and the many other injunctions and Sunna s relating to clothing are further evidence of the importance of dress from the religious, psychological and social points of view.

Social relationships will be disrupted. The responsibilities traditionally held by families, clans, and tribes will be adopted by the state. The individual's sense of responsibility will diminish. This is when the need arises for social services, homes for the elderly, and so on. Cheating in commerce will become the rule, and as part of the people's inability to discern right from wrong, the smooth-talking salesman will be trusted and the honest man distrusted.

Such a society, having discarded much of its religious duties, will have nothing to do but compete in constructing higher buildings and greater projects. 'You shall see the naked, the barefoot, and the shepherds build higher and higher,'[86] says the *ḥadīth*, indicating that there shall be a great amount of wealth coming to the Bedouin.

---

86. Bukhārī, KITĀB AL-IMĀN, 37, and KITĀB AL-FITAN, 35; Muslim, KITĀB AL-IMĀN, 1, 5, and 7.

That the result of this sudden increase in wealth would be nefarious was indicated equally clearly in another *ḥadīth*, 'It is not poverty that I fear for you, but I fear that the world shall open its gates for you, that you shall compete for it as the previous nations competed for it, and that it will destroy you as it has destroyed them.'[87] The destruction in question is obviously religious and moral, having to do with the state of the people on the Day of Judgement.

Nowadays people are respected for their wealth or their achievement in the fields of sports and entertainment. The most famous of all are the football stars and the actors and actresses whose posters adorn the walls of teenage bedrooms. This means that triviality and superficiality have become the order of the day. One of the most disturbing results of this mentality is that people have come to totally misinterpret the saying which enjoins, 'Work for this world as if you were to live forever, and work for the next world as if you were to die tomorrow.' It has always been clear to Muslims that the meaning is that if one were to die tomorrow, one would be very intent indeed on erasing all of one's past sins and accumulating as much merit as possible to protect oneself against the horrors of Hell. There would be very little time for anything else, even for what is usually perceived as vital, such as nourishment and sleep. If on the other hand, one expects to live forever, one would obviously be in no hurry at all to erect palaces, accumulate money, or concentrate all of one's energy on enjoying as much physical pleasure as possible in the shortest time; one would literally have 'all the time in the world.' Unless one has a vested interest in misinterpreting this, it is very difficult to see how it can be understood to enjoin more urgency in achieving worldly aims, but that is exactly how it is misused these days.

Another result of the pervasive degeneration of the nation

87. Bukhārī, KITĀB AL-MAGHĀZĪ, 4016.

is that it will fall prey to the other nations' ambition and greed. 'Nations will invite each other to [eat] you just as those about to eat invite each other to their bowl,' the Prophet ﷺ once said to his Companions. They, the lions of Islam, each one of whom was literally worth an army, were greatly surprised and could think of no explanation for such a strange phenomenon but that the Muslims at that time would be greatly outnumbered. So they asked, 'A very few shall we then be on that day?' And he replied, 'On the contrary, you shall be a multitude, but scum-like, as the scum floating on the surface of the flood waters. God shall remove the fear of you from the hearts of your enemies and cast the weakness into yours. The Companions again asked him about the nature of that 'weakness and he replied, 'The love of this world and the aversion of death.[88] How accurately this describes the Muslims of today: insignificant, weightless, carried by the tides of the times, lacking the moral fibre to accomplish whatever is required, jumping enthusiastically down every lizard hole that the non-believers care to dig for them. This is why 'the sword is no longer used in *Jihād*, because the love of this world and an aversion to death defeat both inward and outward attempts at *Jihād*. The result of these tendencies was described most accurately in the *ḥadīth* stating that the Muslims near the end of time will have, 'tongues as the tongues of Arabs and hearts as the hearts of non-Arabs.'[89] This prophecy, meaning that they shall be so totally westernized that nothing will remain of their heritage but their language, has today come to pass for vast numbers of the Muslim community. They think, dress, behave, and react as westerners, and nothing remains to identify them but their language. Such now is the state of the final prophetic community, the repository of the true inheritance of man.

88. Abū Dāwūd, KITĀB AL-MALĀHIM, 4/111; Aḥmad, 2/359 and 5/278.

89. Aḥmad, 5/340.

The signs we have discussed in this chapter are termed the minor signs of the approach of the Hour. They have all come to pass, down to the smallest detail. There remains nothing but the great conflicts and seditions preceding the appearance of the first of the major signs, namely the Mahdī. The picture we have presented here sometimes draws objections and its implications are brushed aside on the grounds that they are too pessimistic. There are those who claim that it is better to keep one's blinkers on right down to the bottom of the abyss and that technology will provide all the necessary answers. Reality must be faced, however, and it is not for nothing that such an accurate description of the current situation was given by the Prophet of Islam, who is also the Prophet of the End of Time. We must stop harboring naive hopes for sweeping reforms and attend to the business at hand in a realistic manner, tailoring the proposed solution to the size of each problem, with sensible aims and expectations.

The unfolding of time is also the unfolding of the innumerable cosmic rhythms and cycles. Just as men are born, grow to maturity and old age, and then die, so do civilizations, religions, solar systems and galaxies. The signs that we have just mentioned are those of old age and of the decay of the whole of mankind. For the Islamic world, the downward slide has not been uniform. It was interrupted by periods when it was slowed down and at times seemed to have been temporarily reversed, whether in the religious or political order or both. Every now and then a ruler is seen who is a better Muslim than most and during whose reign things tend to take a turn for the better, but events only resume their previous downward course after his passing away. Ṣalāḥ al-Dīn (Saladin) was one such example. More importantly, as the Prophet informed us, 'God shall raise into my nation at the head of each century those who will renew their religion for them,'[90] meaning that these religious leaders will give it a fresh impetus, solve the conceptual problems particular to each epoch and speak to the people in the language best suited to their mentality. The greatest and also the last of such renewers will be the Mahdī.

90. Abū Dāwūd, KITĀB AL-MALĀHIM, 1 and 4/109.

Part Two

The West

4. THE INVERTED CIVILIZATION

INDOCTRINATION

Shall we tell you who will be the greatest losers in their works? Those whose striving goes astray in this life, while they think that theirs are excellent deeds. Those are they who disbelieve in the signs of their Lord and the encounter with Him. Their works have failed. (Qur'ān, 18:103-05)

Successful mass indoctrination today requires very little explicit verbal persuasion. The power of television leads to unquestioning acceptance of all implicit assumptions it bombards its audience with, and ideas which had not existed in previous, more normal societies, are being taken for granted, for example, the promotion of total individual autonomy and independence at the expense of social cohesion and moral values. This amounts to freedom from the need to adhere to any integrative principles and, as we shall demonstrate further on, the right to be disruptive and chaotic according to the very broad limits of what is currently defined as acceptable. This has led the West into positions that diverge so markedly from traditional values as to be their exact opposites in most instances. Man-made theories have filled the vacuum left by a long-defunct Christianity.

The demise of Christianity was due partly to the reaction

against the excesses of the Church and partly to the concerted attacks of those who believed in the supremacy of the human mind and its competence to pass judgment on all matters: material as well as spiritual, secular as well as religious. They began by redefining the spiritual dimension of religion as emotional. This eventually led to the denial of every kind of knowledge except the empirical and, with the discovery of the physiological correlates of emotions, the redefinition of the psychic in purely physical terms. Man was thus reduced to the physical level alone.

Once thinking was freed from the 'shackles' of religion, a multitude of philosophies emerged, the main characteristic of which was rapid changeability. Stability over time came to be considered a sign of weakness. To give one example to illustrate this kind of thinking we shall quote from a recent author who thought that the Chinese, Ottoman and Moghul empires 'all suffered from the consequences of having a centralized authority which insisted upon a uniformity of belief and practice, not only in official state religion, but also in such areas as commercial activities and weapons development.'[91]

The line of thought is that because Europe was poorly organized politically as well as commercially free and competitive, there was a greater possibility for change. 'European societies entered into a constant spiral of economic growth and enhanced military effectiveness which, over time, was to carry them ahead of all other regions of the globe.'[92] From the Islamic point of view, the stability of these three empires, far from being their weakest point, should be regarded as their greatest asset. That they grew old and decayed like everything else on this earth does not detract from the fact that they lasted for centuries; their stability provided the conditions necessary for

91. Paul Kennedy, *The Rise and Fall of the Great Powers: Economic Change and Military Conflict* 1500-2000, Unwin Hyman Ltd, London, 1988, xvi.

92. Ibid., xvii.

the flourishing of societies in which various kinds of sciences, arts, crafts and spirituality existed in harmony. The West, on the contrary, subsists as a monstrous hypertrophy where technology has overshadowed everything else and where inner human development is forcibly arrested at the bestial level, despite vociferous claims to the contrary.

Since nothing in God's creation is entirely good or entirely evil, the Absolute Good being none other than God Himself, all relative beings must exhibit limitations and defects. It is a well known rule that things are to be judged according to their predominant attribute or tendency. Thus, the benevolent aspects of the West should not be denied, but simply put into perspective. Our conclusion is that its evil aspects far outweigh its benevolent ones, and that it is set on a course of self-destruction.

The West is breathlessly attempting to control everything in sight; an impossible task as the variables are innumerable. It is like a train going downhill at full speed. Within each carriage, the passengers feel smugly secure and are intently engaged in making the inside of the carriage ever more comfortable and pleasurable. The driver feels in control and sends reassuring messages to the passengers despite the fact that whenever he attempts to reduce speed the brakes do not respond. It never occurs to him to try to halt the train, for he still does not suspect that he has lost his brakes and all control over the engine. The crash is inevitable, but very few are those whose vision is clear enough to see it coming. They attempt to divert the others' attention from their immediate pleasures and warn them of what is coming but their words remain unheard till *when the earth has taken on its glitter and has decked itself fair and its inhabitants think they have power over it, Our command comes upon it by night or day and We make it stubble, as though yesterday it flourished not* (10:24).

POLUTION

Nowadays everybody knows or ought to know that nature's way of protecting itself against disequilibrium is by means of ecosystems which effectively dispose of pollutants and thus keep the environment healthy. For example, if the organic waste produced by a primitive village is dumped into the nearby river and the river is examined a few hundred yards downstream, the water will be found to have regained its cleanliness and limpidity. Each of these systems however, has a capacity which, if exceeded, leads to its failure and the accumulation of pollutants. Many rivers and lakes in the West today are dead, since their degree of pollution no longer allows fish to survive. Even those which still have some life are health hazards since they are polluted with pesticides, sewage, and industrial waste such as mercury. These substances may become concentrated in the food chain and cause epidemics of food poisoning. Another example of disequilibrium is the disruption of the balance of gases in the atmosphere which is dependent on the earth's 'green mantle' and the ocean plankton which are the planet's oxygen producers and carbon dioxide consumers. Deforestation and the destruction of plankton due to the chemical pollution of the oceans have already caused an increase in carbon dioxide and a reduction in oxygen. This is constantly aggravated by the massive consumption of oxygen by internal combustion engines, factories and jet aircraft. To obtain enough wood to print the multitude of newspapers, magazines, and books that are produced every day, this civilization is depriving itself of the very oxygen that sustains its life.

Another result of the disturbance of the balance of gases in the atmosphere is that the heat absorbed by the earth from the sun is not re-radiated outwardly as it should be: heat is thus stored in the system and the temperature rises steadily, producing the 'greenhouse effect.'

Yet another disturbance is the now notorious defect in the ozone layer and the resulting passage of excessive amounts of ultraviolet rays.

Food, a vital element, has also suffered grievously from the drive to mass produce at all costs. Meat is produced in artificial conditions that are certainly extremely stressful to the animals. Stress is known to disturb many systems in the body, the best known of which are the suprarenal glands which hypertrophy and secrete an excessive amount of adrenaline. Other hormones are added to the artificially fattening fodder and the end result of this is extremely suspect. Cattle are fed their dead brothers so as not to 'waste' a penny, thereby turning herbivores into carnivores and spreading mad cow disease. Fruits and vegetables are likewise sprayed with herbicides, pesticides, hormones and so on. The owners of such enterprises evidently claim that it has never been proved conclusively that any of these things is harmful. The same argument is used again and again to justify practices which at first sight seem very deleterious indeed. These delaying tactics insure that by the time any such thing is proved and they are exposed, the proprietors would have already made a substantial profit. One well documented example is the discovery in the 1950s that not only did all those working with asbestos eventually develop a malignant tumour of the pleural coverings of the lungs, but that all their wives also suffered the same fate, which was probably due to the inhalation of asbestos while ironing their husbands' clothes. The scientist who made this discovery was silenced by the political weight of the industry and nothing changed for the workers and their families for years. As for salt water, apart from the substantial pesticide pollution which led to the finding that DDT was present in Antarctic seals, its main pollutant is oil: oil is spilled at terminals while being pumped ashore from tankers, waste oil is discharged by ships, oil is spilled by damaged tankers, and more seriously, oil leaks from underwater wells. The sight of seagulls covered in oil and lying dead on seashores has become a familiar television image.

Another major problem is the promotion of nuclear energy as an alternative to oil. The bad faith of government agencies as regards this subject has become notorious. Leaks from supposedly safe plants have occurred much more frequently than is officially admitted. Accidents were inevitable and anyone not suffering from the delusion of invincibility and infallibility could have predicted that tankers would sink and nuclear plants leak. How many Chernobyl disasters are required to awaken them? Nuclear testing, radioactive waste, and the prospective use of nuclear weapons in warfare, even of a limited kind, as well as by terrorists, complete the picture.

Other issues of importance are thermal and noise pollution, smog, earthquakes due to the erection of dams, the explosive increase in carcinogenic substances, and the extermination of whole species of animals because of induced changes in their habitat or because of their market value.

The pattern that emerges from the study of each of these topics is that the West is ever hastening to use new devices before considering the implications and possible dangers. Scientists are often heard to repeat that they are simply researchers and thus the onus for the rational use of what they invent falls upon others. This is blatant nonsense. Anyone as intelligent as Einstein should have known what politicians would use his discoveries for. Furthermore, when problems arise due to technology they attempt to solve them in the same manner, that is, by devising half-baked solutions that are sure to produce more problems. Thus, for each problem solved another dozen are generated. Since scientific research is yielding more and more fragmented, equivocal, and unwieldy information, scientists are specializing more and more in lesser and lesser areas. They thus lose all ability to see an overall picture and science is thus irredeemably divorced from wisdom. How are people to be judged who are intelligent enough to embark on the so-called conquest of space, yet are irresponsible enough to use that selfsame intelligence to invent virulent strains of microorganisms capable of wiping out whole populations in the event of armed conflict? *Corruption has appeared in the land and sea, for that men's own hands have earned* (30:41).[93]

SOCIAL DISORDER

Industrialization uproots people from their villages and destroys their social support networks; social cohesion is lost in the anonymity of city life and the traditional responsibilities of the community toward each of its members is passed on to the state. In place of the normal support, based on ties of kinship, we have man-made institutions trying to come up with ad hoc solutions. In other words, the state, having created the problem, then proceeds to interfere with the victims along whichever line of thought is in vogue at that particular moment, creating a highly unstable situation.

Urban living itself is so fraught with problems that the reasonable thing to do, for everyone able to afford it, has become to live in the suburbs or rush out into the countryside at each opportunity. High-rise concrete blocks and matchbox apartments, scurrying about in cars, buses, and planes, being subject to rush hours, deadlines, pressures to produce, and competition of all sorts have evident adverse effects. The alienation of city life and the ignominy of becoming a more-or-less nameless unit in a production line lead to many kinds of abnormal behaviour in attempts to alleviate this estrangement.[94] It also seems that the West, with its greater disruption

93. It is worth noting how the Qur'ān speaks of the corruption of the sea at a time when it was totally inconceivable that human powers to corrupt could become so pervasive.

94. The official suicide rate in Ireland increased markedly between 1970 and

of social cohesion, is less immune to the evils of urbanization than other societies.[95]

One of the greatest and most irremediable disasters of modern society is the destruction of the normal role of women as mothers and wives and its replacement with an ill-defined, ill-assimilated equality with men that has blurred the distinctions between the two sexes and relieved each of their specific responsibilities without offering a viable alternative. Western women are persuaded that they are being held down, trampled underfoot, despised, and iniquitously held captive in lowly roles. Mothering is devalued in favor of career achievement and pleasure seeking. By contrast, women never felt oppressed in Muslim societies until early in this century when, under the influence of Western education, the more affluent strata of society began to lead a dual life: a 'liberated' one in Europe, and a more conventional one at home. They then began agitating for more ' freedom, clamouring to remove their traditional veils and to be given equal chance in the labour market. The wheel has now turned full circle and young girls all over the Islamic world are reverting to dressing modestly, this time with full freedom, and often in opposition to the wishes of their Westernized parents. It should be said that in reality women were much less highly regarded in the West than in Muslim societies, which might explain the violence of their reaction to traditional Muslim women and also the lack of enthusiasm which most Muslim women exhibit in following the western model, contrary to the current popular Muslim practice of blind

1985... Possible reasons for this change include an increase in "anomie" shown by a rise in the rates of crime, illegitimacy, and admissions to hospital for alcoholism, a decline in social cohesion revealed by a fall in the marriage rate and a rise in the number of separated couples, and an increase in unemployment. (Brit. J. of Psychiatry, 57 (1990), 533-38.)

95. According to the *New York Post* (November 26, 1971), Tokyo, which has a greater population and higher density, had five times fewer murders than New York City in 1970.

imitation of the West. We shall discuss the status accorded to women in Islam in a subsequent section.

An example of the way in which socially cohesive forces are destroyed in the name of individual freedom is that of the changing meaning and function of jealousy. The Islamic concept of jealousy, based on the Prophet's teachings, is that jealousy is socially desirable to the extent that it provides the motivating force for people of both sexes to protect their families, and in this as in all things the middle way is to be sought. Too little of it in a man denotes lack of virility and too much leads to blameworthy tyranny.

What has happened to jealousy in the West? 'Jealousy,' writes a Western psychiatrist, 'despite its attendant darker side, was accorded a role in preserving social esteem in societies ruled principally by concepts of honor.'[96] It is now recognized that honour is no longer a social force and the loss of the concept of honour has led to a redefinition of the concept of jealousy. 'The changing construction of jealousy in Western societies has transformed a socially sanctioned response to infidelity into a form of personal pathology which is the mere outward expression of immaturity, possessiveness, and insecurity.'[97] Let us note that the kind of jealousy equated here with immaturity, possessiveness and insecurity is not the pathological kind but the kind that is still considered quite appropriate in less disordered societies. What is being said here is that to be considered mature and emotionally secure one should allow one's spouse to enjoy all kinds of extramarital activities and remain totally unconcerned. A study of the same subject in America is then quoted as follows:

> Stearns (1989) points out in his history of jealousy in America that the 19th-century was riven by conflicting influences on jealousy. On the one hand urbanization broke down the traditional small com-

96. P. E. Mullen, 'Jealousy: The Pathology of Passion,' British Journal of Psychiatry, 158 (1991), 598.

97. Ibid.

> munities with their mutual enforcement of fidelity by public scrutiny. America gradually abandoned the institutional enforcement of sexual fidelity through its laws against adultery. At the same time the opportunities for romantic and sexual encounters increased and prostitution flourished. Equally, the rise of commercial codes of behavior made concerns for honor seem anachronistic.[98]

The author then goes on to say:

> Current Western society reflects the influence of the market freedom, of democratization, and of the notion of freedom expressed through individual rights. Modernism leaves no place either for jealousy's claim for exclusivity, which offends against individual rights and liberal notions of freedom, or for the jealous person, who is an emotional bankrupt in the marketplace of love. Equally, the acceptance of ideas about individual rights as the final arbiter of the good in our society marginalizes any claims made on behalf of moral or ethical imperatives which infringe such notions.[99]

It cannot be put more plainly than that. Honour has been replaced by the market-place mentality and ethical and moral considerations should not stand in the way of any individual wishing to give free rein to his bestial appetites. The collective good is no longer marketable as a motive force for discipline and self-restraint.

A disordered society without any higher principles other than the explicit aim to satisfy as many of its members' physical appetites as possible cannot control deviant tendencies. It has no option but to legitimize them. Identity crises are a product of the modern world. In a traditional environment where everyone knows his rights and his duties, where roles are well defined, and where the notion of an afterlife still exercises some influence, such crises need never arise.

---

98. Ibid. See also R. N. Stearns, *Jealousy: The Evolution of an Emotion in American History*, New York University Press, New York, 1989.

99. Mullen, *Jealousy*, 598.

PSYCHOLOGY

Modern psychology, as part of Western civilization, suffers from the same fundamental defect just cited, namely the absence of any higher integrative principles. The consequence of this is again the lack of a theoretical framework, based on the certainty of revealed knowledge, capable of accommodating observational data and synthesizing it into a practically-useful coherent whole. One result has been the equation of the mind with the brain and the emotions with their autonomic correlates. Another result is the emergence of a vast number of very dissimilar theories, each based on limited observations and extended by sheer force of imagination to cover the whole gamut of human experience.[100] The profusion of theories in circulation today is itself proof enough that none of them has succeeded in offering a sufficiently comprehensive view of man. It is true that many theorists have provided valid partial insights into specific areas of behaviour, but few have been objective enough to resist the temptation of extending the explanatory powers of their observations to include everything, thus founding a 'school,' to the tenets of which 'disciples' cling tenaciously, reacting to criticism in much the same way as religious fanatics do. In other words, they have replaced Christianity and Judaism with psychoanalysis and behaviorism. The fact that these, together with evolution, were the actual replacement of religion was proven by their propagation as established facts to the masses. Their superficial and reductionist style appealed to the majority, as did the pleasurable freedom from religious commitment they bestowed upon their adherents.

The intention here is neither to review the history of modern psychology in detail nor to discuss each school individually, but rather to indicate some of their weaknesses and provide some of the

100. The most patently absurd example was the attempt to explain religion on the basis of laboratory work on pigeons!

keys necessary for evaluating current theories. The coming remarks, together with the principles and criteria discussed throughout the book, should be sufficient to place the whole field of modern psychology in its proper perspective. Although we deal only with the clinical kind of psychology, other kinds such as social, educational, and industrial psychology can easily be subjected to the same process.

The two most notorious examples to illustrate the points we have just made are those of Sigmund Freud and Carl Jung. Both, the first a Jew, the second a Christian, shared a desire to detach themselves from their respective religions and to redefine the human situation using their intelligence as the only criterion. Both constructed highly complicated but mutually incompatible theories which claimed to explain almost everything, including things which had for centuries been considered by the sages of every civilization to fall within the spiritual not the psychic domain. Both claimed to explain religion in terms of their theories: Freud, the more materialistic of the two, by relegating it to a nebulous unconscious driven by blind bestial instincts; and Jung by producing a pseudo-spirituality immediately recognizable for the parody that it is by its relegation of the 'archetypes' to the collective unconscious, that is, by redefining the highest spiritual level as the lowest stratum in the human psyche.

SCIENCE AS RELIGION

Man cannot live without some kind of religion: even those who hold that there is no such thing as religion merely substitute one set of beliefs for another. Religion consists in a doctrine which explains what man is, his position within the universe, and his relationship with the Absolute. It offers a law which regulates man's transactions with his environment, and beyond that, it offers a method of spiritual ascent. It should always be remembered that the memory of the lost paradise lingers on within men as does the feeling of the upward pull of the spirit. When Christianity lost its credibility and hence its powers to explain, it was simply replaced by the more materialistic alternatives on offer. Thus instead of seeking to reach the real paradise, people busied themselves with obtaining as much pleasure from the only paradise left to them—that of immediate enjoyment in this life. And instead of striving along the path of spiritual ascent, they chose the cruder and more materialistic alternative to satisfy this need, which was to reach for the moon. The explanations of religion were replaced by scientific theories, with mere conjecture being presented as fact and held onto as tenaciously as any religious belief ever was. The most notorious example is, of course, the theory of evolution. Despite the large number of people who have attempted to demonstrate that the scientific community was equally divided between supporters and foes, popular mythology accepts it as a proven fact, and scientists from other disciplines readily use the concept as categorically as they use directly observable data. Belief in science is currently perceived as conferring the right to be sceptical of everything, including science, and as release from the obligation to strive for the truth.

Dr. Albert Ellis, an American psychologist who originated a reasonably successful form of psychotherapy that he labelled 'Rational Emotive Therapy,' writes:

> The idea that certain people are bad or wicked springs from the ancient theological doctrine of free will, which assumes that every person has the freedom to act 'rightly' or 'wrongly' in relation to some absolute standard of truth and justice ordained by 'God' or the 'natural law'; and that if anyone uses his 'free will' to behave 'wrongly' he is a wicked sinner. This doctrine has no scientific foundation because its key terms—including 'absolute truth,' 'God,' 'free will,' and 'natural law'—are purely definitional and can neither be

proven nor disproven in empirical scientific terms.[101]

This kind of argument is fairly widespread in the West and reveals the contradictions inherent in such pseudo-objectivity. Denying the Absolute must surely also mean denying oneself the right to speak in such absolute terms. To think of proof as only possible in purely scientific terms is to attribute to science a competence far exceeding its quite limited territory. It is to be so hypnotized by science that sight is lost of the fact that it is valid only in what pertain to the material level, and that also in a very relative way. It would have been more 'rational' to think that proof should be adequate to the level of what needs to be proved. Intelligible things require intelligible proof and spiritual things require spiritual proof. The fact that the West has lost the ability to accept spiritual proof neither renders the spiritual dimension non-existent nor does it affect the validity of such proof at its own level. That they cannot prove God scientifically merely proves that He is not material enough to be measured; to conclude that He therefore does not exist is patently absurd. Now what if He did? What if those millions of people who lived throughout the centuries believing in a life to come were not so naive and backward after all? What of the inertia and complacency of those who do not even wish to find out? Pleasure seeking and the wish to achieve are basic human traits; however, the West has substituted immediate and lowly pleasures for those of Paradise and the spirit, and achievement in terms of income and social status for spiritual growth.

There are a few people in the West who are aware that theirs is indeed a precarious situation and who have some degree of sincerity in wishing to find a way out. They will first of all have to disentangle themselves from the current myths which shape their mentality, and they will then be faced with the myriad of pseudo-religions which abound in the West today, and nowhere more so than

101. Albert Ellis, *Reason and Emotion in Psychotherapy*, Citadel Press, NJ, 1962, 65.

in America. Some of these are parodies of true traditions, others are invented from moment to moment as the situation requires, and there are even some which are based on science fiction. Very few indeed are those who are able to see through such mirages and keep their feet firmly on the ground.

THE IMPOSTOR

Judaism and Christianity both agree with Islam in affirming a downward trend for humanity which is to continue until the cataclysms heralding Doomsday. Sometime during the late stages of this process, the Antichrist shall appear, who is not only the epitome of all evil but also the inverted image of Jesus, may peace be upon him, whom he will claim to personify. The Prophet, may God's blessings and peace be on him, called him the 'Impostor' (*al-Dajjāl*) since his characteristic attribute will be relabeling good as evil and evil as good, Heaven as Hell and Hell as Heaven, himself as the Christ and Christ as the Antichrist.

And this is precisely what the West has already succeeded in doing. They have redefined the human being by bringing his physical form to the fore and denying his spirit, redefining him thus as an animal; and they have set the stage for putting everything to the service of the body and thinking solely in material terms. Whereas all religions say that man is degenerating, the West claims that, on the contrary, he is improving by the day; with the implication that they are now far more 'advanced,' far more clever and mature than anyone in the past. This evidently gives them the right to dismiss lightly the Prophets and sages of old and their timeless wisdom and speak of them in condescending and derogatory terms. Religion has been redefined as superstition, and the life-to-come as a childish belief deriving from an inability to face reality. Miraculous events are no more than trickery, hypnosis or self-deluding fantasies. Alcohol, gambling, and usury are socially condoned practices. Chastity has now become a charge that most youngsters are anxious to avoid. Homosexuality has already been legalized. It is legal to have intercourse with any number of males, females, or even animals, but it is illegal to have two officially recognized wives, each enjoying, together with her children, full legal rights. More than half the men and women in the West have extramarital affairs, a good proportion having multiple affairs.[102] The range of what is defined as normal is rapidly being extended to exclude nothing. The death penalty has been almost totally abolished. This means that the person who kills another is certain to survive and have a sporting chance of being let off for good behaviour after an acceptable number of years in a fairly comfortable prison. Thus the murderer is guaranteed the right to live' that same right he has deprived his victim of!

The following passage, admitting to the wilful madness of such a system, was taken from a review of a book written by J. Gilligan, an American forensic psychiatrist:

> ...the U.S.A. which is massively more violent than any other democracy and every other economically developed nation (its prison population is over 2 million - nearly 1% of the population), and just happens to be by far the singular dominant nation of the world in economic and material terms. He [i.e. Gilligan] quotes Currie (1985): 'we have the level of criminal violence we do because we have arranged our social and economic life [as we have]...the brutality and violence of American life are a signal that there are profound social costs to maintain these arrangements.' We have decided that we prefer this to a far less violent alternative.[103]

---

102. Annette Lawson, *Adultery: An Analysis of Love and Betrayal*, Basic Books, New York, 1988, 46.

103. C. Cordess, book review of J. Gilligan's *Violence: Reactions on Our Deadliest Epidemic* (Jessica Kingsley, London, 1999), British Journal of Psychiatry, 178 (2001), 186.

Then there is the clamour for human rights, which all hinges on who is defined as human and consequently as having rights. The Americans manifestly denied the Red Indians human status, and thus were able to exterminate systematically whole nations of them. The Spanish did the same in Latin America. Hitler also refused human status to the mentally-ill, the subnormal, even before turning his demonic attention to the Poles, then to many ethnic groups including the Jews and the gypsies. He was thus able to massacre them not only without internal opposition, but by recruiting some of the Èlite of German society. However, let us not forget that the euthanasia program came into being long before the Nazis came to power. For example, in 1922, Gerhard Hoffman laid before the Reichstag a plan for the mass extermination of the mentally ill, the terminally-ill, the exhausted, the crippled and incurably-ill children. A decade later this was adopted as official policy and, with the help of numerous physicians and nurses, 200,000 persons were murdered between 1939 and 1945.[104] And let us also not forget that Hitler, Stalin, Milosevic and their likes are nothing if not products of Western civilization.

The Huns and Mongols were brutal indeed as they established their military supremacy over conquered territories, yet their worst excesses amount to little when compared objectively to the mass atrocities committed by this civilization, for they, at least, were never genocidal. This is not to deny that there are millions of humane and compassionate people in the West, but the very fact that they accept such people as Hitler and Milosevic for leaders must indicate something. The behind-the-scenes machinations of their now-dominant world system in bringing Third World Hitlers and Milosevic's to power is also proverbial. It is not sufficient for humane people

104. See Michael Burleigh, *Death and Deliverance: Euthanasia in Germany, 1990-1945*, Cambridge University Press, Cambridge, 1994.

in the West simply to dissociate themselves from all of this mentally. The best elements in Western society are kept away from power, yet the duplicity of those actually wielding it is no longer capable of being effectively camouflaged. One must be blinded with prejudice not to see that, as nations, rather than individuals, the West very often says one thing and does the opposite. Grand proclamations of human rights are made and used as smokescreens behind which are carried out their real intentions, whether these be to prop up a repressive totalitarian regime or to bring down another that is anti-Western, to justify massive military intervention in Kuwait or total inertia in Rwanda, and so on.

What more evidence is needed to show that the West is actually an 'inverted' civilization? We have mentioned previously how Freud closed all the upper gates by denying that there was a spirit and dismissing religion as something springing from the human unconscious, while opening all the lower gates by trying to bring to the surface the lowest tendencies in human beings. This was a very effective way indeed of shutting man from heavenly influences and leaving him defenseless before demonic ones. We also made mention of Jung's definition of the archetypes as something belonging to a hypothetical collective unconscious, that is, archetypes as situated below, whereas the true archetypes belong to the highest spiritual level.

The Devil and his influences are denied as myth while at the same time his handiwork is everywhere manifest, and even openly promoted and familiarized through such mediums as popular demonic films, music and even cartoons. God is likewise relegated to myth, while the reflection of His Attributes such as Truth, Justice and Mercy in human society is everywhere touted but are manifestly missing. It remains to say that from the Islamic point of view, Western civilization is the inevitable last stage in human degeneracy. The downward trend has been progressing for thousands of years, but its acceleration has now become insane. To reach rock-bottom in this process there had to emerge a civilization totally cut off from all spirituality and all higher principles, leading to chaos at all levels together with the inability to recognize such chaos for what it really is. Such a civilization must offer the appearance of unparalleled excellence in everything material and to have gone such a long way in the process of redefinition and inversion as to deprive its people of all power of discernment. This sets the stage for the crowning event in this process, the appearance of the Impostor. He is described in *ḥadīth* as able to move across the face of the earth as swiftly as 'rain-clouds carried by the wind,' and to ride on a mount so great that 'the distance between its ears is forty cubits.' Furthermore, his voice will carry so far that it will be heard by 'the people of the East and those of the West.' These descriptions are nowadays easily translatable into currently existing technological devices. We can assert with confidence that the West is now ready for the Impostor. People are mentally imprisoned in the tangible world and this is precisely the dimension that the Impostor will be able to master and he shall show them such wonders in that they will readily accept whatever claims he shall wish to make.

It may appear from our previous depiction of the degeneration of Muslim societies and our description in this chapter of the West that they stand equal in this respect. This is not so. The kind of inversion that we have just described is something that has already been consummated and normalized in the West, whereas among Muslims, although the trend is similar, it is much less widespread and is still recognized as abnormal.

Part Three

Normative Islamic Values

5. WHAT IS A NORM?

NORMS

The Islamic definition of the norm is radically different from that of the West. What is normal in Western terms is what is present in the average man in the street, that is, the majority of the population. This view is garbed in scientific respectability by means of statistics: the notorious bell shaped curve where individuals positioned at either tail are considered abnormal. It is nothing less than the legitimization of mediocrity.

By contrast, the norm in Islamic terms is nothing less than the original or primordial nature of man, or his *fiṭrā*. *We have indeed created man in the best constitution* (95:4), says the Qur'ān. The reason why this is termed 'norm' and not 'ideal' is that, far from being a mere theoretical or hypothetical construction, this pattern was actually lived in Madina in the early days of Islam and still is, to this very day, by those who strive to realize it in full. The norm in Islam is thus the Sunna of the Prophet, may God's blessings be upon him, and that of the Companions and Followers.[105] The Sunna represents

105. These three generations were specifically mentioned by the Prophet ﷺ and this is why they are to this day greatly revered and taken as models by most Muslims. The *ḥadīth* states, 'The best generation is my generation, then that

the very perfection of human behavior and anything less than that is considered abnormal. Consequently, the Westerner stagnates in the smug satisfaction that is mediocrity, because it is shared by the majority of his contemporaries, is normality itself. But the true Muslim, aware of how short he has fallen from the norm that should be his by birthright, can never allow himself to stagnate and feel comfortable and 'well adjusted' in his imperfection, but rather is obliged to strive constantly to regain what he feels he has lost. The farther the Muslim is from understanding normality as defined by the Sunna and the closer he is to conceiving of it in the Western manner, the less motivated he is to strive for real superiority.

The Islamic norm, as lived by the Prophet Muḥammad ﷺ covers a vast range of human behaviour. For besides his function as Divine Messenger and legislator, which is exclusive and inimitable, he also lived the roles of orphan, shepherd, merchant, father, adoptive father, grandfather, warrior, political leader, and husband of women both older and younger than himself. At times he was poor to the extent of not having cooked food in his house for weeks on end, while at other times he was rich to the extent of being able to give away a valley full of sheep. He survived mortal dangers, plots, and formidable hardships, saw all his children but one die before him, began his emigration as a fugitive hiding in a cave, and eventually returned to Makka as a conqueror. This, together with what is on record concerning the pattern of behaviour of his Companions and his approval or criticism of them, leaves almost nothing of what human beings think, feel, say or do without a clear model to emulate.

---

which will follow, then that which will follow.' Bukhārī, KITĀB FAḌL AṢḤĀB AL-NABĪ, I.

INDIVIDUAL VALUES

The values that have been nurtured in Muslims for centuries may be divided, for the sake of clarity, to correspond to the spiritual, psychic, physical and social levels. This section deals with the first three as aspects of the individual, including what is currently termed as 'personality' in Western psychology.

(A) Spiritual Principles

In Islamic terms, each person's worth is primarily a function of his knowledge of God and revelation to the extent that this knowledge is assimilated and effectively shapes his cognition, emotion and behavior.

Revelation teaches the science of *tawḥīd*, or unification, which is the science of the Divine Essence, Attributes and Acts of God, and the consequences of this knowledge upon our conception of existence and our behavior in this world. Spirituality is not a fuzzy catch-all term for every in tense emotional or non-physical experience, but instead refers to this Prophetic legacy of knowledge and behavior.

As we have mentioned earlier, the Divine Attributes are usually categorized as Attributes of Beauty (*Jamāl*) and Majesty (*Jalāl*). The first include all those Attributes that are derived from mercy and compassion, such as forgiveness, forbearance, responsiveness, liberality, guidance, support, succor and so on. The second include such Attributes as might, justice, retaliation, omnipotence and so on. The Qur'ān clearly indicates that when the Divine aspects are turned toward creation, the Attributes of Beauty take precedence over those of Majesty: *My Mercy encompasses everything* (7:156). And the *ḥadīth qudsī*[106] states, 'My Mercy precedes My Wrath.'[107] This is

106. A *ḥadīth qudsī* or holy utterance is defined as a tradition in which God speaks in the first person on the tongue of His Prophet ﷺ.

107. Bukhārī, KITĀB AL-TAWḤĪD, 55, KITĀB BADA' AL-KHALQ, 1; and Muslim, KITĀB AL-TAWBA, 14.

also the obvious implication of *The All-Merciful, on the Throne, has established Himself* (20:5).

Al-Rahman, the All-Merciful, is He whose mercy envelops every single creature in the universe: men and beasts, believers and unbelievers alike. This all-inclusive mercy has many aspects, one of which is that of the Provider, the Arabic term al-Razzāq, which clearly conveys the idea of persistent continuous solicitude. This Attribute is that of Him who is the guarantor of the fulfillment of needs such as, for example, sustenance, shelter and mating. Another aspect is that of the Responsive (al-Mujīb) Who is willing to respond to His servants' pleas and prayers: *Your Lord has said: 'Call upon Me And I shall answer you'* (40:60). Yet another is the Infinitely Rich (al-Ghanī) Who is also the Enricher (al-Mughnī) the One Who frees His servants from relying on other created beings.

Within this surrounding envelope of Divine mercy there is a dimension of depth that is selective and extends into the life to come. This is designated by the Attribute, al-Raḥīm, usually rendered in English as the Compassionate, which does no justice to the difference of meaning between it and al-Raḥmān. Al-Raḥīm is the One who dispenses the mercies of right-guidance, spiritual knowledge and the eternal felicity of the Garden.

As for the Attributes of Majesty, they are to be seen in the many limitations that created beings are subject to, such as the inevitability of perpetual change, which includes the outward and inward fluctuations that occur every instant, as well as major changes of state such as death. Other limitations include the inability to gratify one's wishes either instantaneously or in full and to escape losses, calamities, injustice, tyranny, and so on. The world is a constant interplay between Majesty or Rigour and Beauty or Mercy, whereas in the life to come mercy manifests itself in its purest form in Paradise, and Rigour manifests itself in its purest form in Hell. This knowledge forms the realm in which spirituality exists, that is, the states and stations of direct experience of God and their consequent actions, leading to further experience and action engendering ever deepening understanding. These paths of intimacy are well travelled and documented and remain open to sincere persons till the end of time. Some of these basic states are described below.

Knowledge of the Attributes of Beauty induces in the soul such states as hope (*rajā'*) for God's forgiveness, generosity and protection, as well as gratitude for what has already been granted and the confident expectation of further beneficence. The result of these is that the love of God wells up in the heart; as the *ḥadīth* describes it, 'Love God for the gifts that He bestows upon you, love me for the love of God, and love my family for the love of me.'[108] There is a higher love than that, which is to love God for no reason other than His absolute perfection, since the human soul was made to love and be ever-attracted to perfection; and God's is the only true perfection: all other perfections being nothing but relative reflections of that perfection in the created worlds.

The love of God is a driving force that generates such spiritual gains as total reliance on Him (*tawakkul*), which is to commit oneself unconditionally to Him and to abandon hope in created beings. It is to perform one's duties to perfection while expecting neither reward nor appreciation from ephemeral beings. It is also to separate the act from its result since the act is from the creature but the result from God, which means that the same act may bring different results if God so wills: *My success is but from God* (11:88). The habitual manner of perceiving cause and effect relationships in this world induces many people to depend on them. They then forget that unforeseen factors may enter into any such sequence and produce an altogether different result, or that the physical laws of causality may

108. Tirmidhī, KITĀB AL-MANĀQIBĪ, 31.

be superseded by those from a higher world or suspended by their Maker.

Another related spiritual gain is contentment, *riḍa'*, which is the state of maintaining one's joyful serenity in the face of adversity in the knowledge that only God is capable of giving and withholding. His is the only power in the universe, and He is the All-Merciful. The Prophet ﷺ said to Ibn ʿAbbās one day,

> Boy, I will teach you a few words: guard [your duties toward] God and He will guard you; guard [your duties toward] God and you will find Him before you. When you ask, ask only God, and when you seek help, seek only God's help. And know that if the whole nation were to unite to benefit you, they would benefit you only with something that God has [already] decreed for you; and were they to unite to harm you, they would harm you only with something that God has [already] decreed for you. The pens have been lifted and the parchments have dried.[109]

The consequence of this understanding is that one neither pleases anyone at the cost of God's displeasure, nor praises anyone to obtain what are actually God's favours nor blames anyone for what God has chosen to withhold. When you perceive the Divine ability as the only power that exists, you neither fear any man enough to try to please him at the cost of committing a sin, nor attribute whatever good comes to you to the created beings by whose mediation it was sent, nor credit created beings with the power to withhold that which is yours by Divine decree. But it must be understood that this state by no means prompts one to act with ingratitude towards one's benefactors, quite to the contrary, for 'He has not thanked God who does not thank men.'[110] And it must be remembered that these are not mere mental constructs we are discussing, but profound states of being reflected in action.

109. Tirmidhī, KITĀB AL-QIYĀMA, 59; Aḥmad, 1/293 and 307.

110. Tirmidhī, KITĀB AL-BIRR, 35; Abū Dāwūd, KITĀB AL-ADAB, 11.

Similarly, we are enjoined to defend ourselves as best we can against those who wish us harm, yet one must never lose sight of the reality of things, which is that no harm may reach anyone save with Divine permission. One must always rely upon the Divine wisdom which underlies the secret of destiny and which is the Divine ability to put everything in the most suitable place, at the most suitable time and in the most suitable manner. The Prophet ﷺ said, 'God, in His equity and justice, has made joy and relief the consequence of contentment; and worry and sorrow the consequence of discontent.[111]

For a believer, maintaining one's serenity in the face of adversity is rooted in the knowledge that when a believer suffers hardship it is 'an atonement and a purification for him, unless he attributes what ails him to other than God and prays to other than God for relief.'[112] It is understanding that afflictions are but manifestations of the Attributes of majesty and rigour. One ought then also to regard natural phenomena such as floods, hurricanes and earthquakes, and human phenomena such as wars in the same manner. Serenity is maintained through the knowledge that, When God loves certain people he tests them; those who are content He is content with them, and those who are discontent He is discontented with them.[113] This is why, when the Prophet, may God's blessings and peace be on him, was asked who among men suffered the greatest hardships, he replied, 'The Prophets, then those who most resemble them, and so on. People are afflicted in proportion to the strength of their faith: those whose faith is strong suffer severe hardships, while those whose faith is weak suffer lesser hardships. A man may suffer [successive] hardships until he comes to walk the

111. Tirmidhī, KITĀB AL-ZUHD, 57; Ibn Māja, KITĀB AL-FITAN, 23.

112. Aḥmad, 3/159.

113. Tirmidhī, KITĀB AL-ZUHD, 57; Ibn Māja, KITĀB AL-FITAN, 23.

earth with no sins remaining attached to him.'[114] Again, this is why he also said that a believer's condition is always good: when he is granted a favor he thanks his Lord for it, and when he is afflicted he endures patiently and prays for relief. Such a man is never a loser: *We shall surely try you with something of fear and hunger, and diminution of goods and lives and fruits; yet give good tidings to these who are patient, who, when afflicted with hardship; say: 'We belong to God and to Him we shall return'* (2:155-57).

When perceived in this manner, adversity induces emotions different from the usual resentment or mindless rage of man against his destiny. Adversity is seen as purification from the effects of sinful or heedless behavior on the heart, then as purification from egocentric and individualistic tendencies, then as a necessary preparation for higher spiritual gains. A servant whom God has predestined to reach a certain [spiritual] rank and who fails to reach it by his efforts will have God test him in his body, possessions, or children; if he endures patiently, he is granted his predestined rank by God, August and Exalted is He. Knowledge of Divine Rigour induces in the heart the fear of God and stimulates one's vigilance, with the realization that He knows every thought, word, and act, and that there shall be a reaction in kind to each. At a higher level than fear of retaliation or chastisement is awe before the immensity of the Divine Might. It has often been said that the believer soars toward his Lord on the two wings of hope and fear, and that they must counterbalance each other to provide flight.

Let us now examine the concept of 'self-esteem' in the light of this kind of knowledge. To the disbeliever, self-esteem is based on his opinion of himself and what he perceives as others' opinion of him. The believer, on the other hand, bases his self-esteem on the human race's ultimate equality in their utter dependence on Divine

114. Bukhārī, KITĀB AL-MARDA, 3; Tirmidhī, KITĀB AL-ZUHD, 57.

power to sustain their very existence. For were this sustaining power, this *qayyumiyya*, to be withdrawn, all would vanish into immediate nothingness. Thus, being a slave of God is common to both beggars and kings, leaving no reason for kings to feel superior or for beggars to feel inferior. Both are nothing before the Absolute, their real worth depending on their purity of heart, not the richness of their clothes. This is nowhere better demonstrated than in the yearly gathering of ḥajj on the plain of ʿArafāt, where all stand feeble and destitute, begging for mercy, all outward signs of social status removed, leaving nothing but the acute feeling of total helplessness and dependence upon God's compassion.

Self confidence, if based on personal achievement, is nothing but an illusion that can easily be shattered, since achievement is but a free gift, a Divine grace, and, when misused, liable to be withdrawn. Confidence in God, on the other hand, is the calm certainty that as He has given before, He will give again, and as He has protected before, He will protect again, and as He has responded before, He will respond again. Just as worldly self-confidence increases with the repeated experience of success, confidence in God increases with the repeated experience of Divine responsiveness and solicitude. It ultimately leads to reliance on God in preference to created beings and one's own abilities, and to the piercing of the veil of material causes and effects. Imperturbability is the characteristic of those who achieve this condition, whereas anxiety and futile agitation remain that of those who do not.

(B) Virtues and Vices

Character is traditionally described by Muslim authors as a collection of traits which are then classified into two groups according to their conformity or opposition to the Prophetic norm and hence their consequences in the hereafter. The first group consists of 'saving things,' *al-munjiyāt*, and the second of 'ruinous things,' *al-*

muhlikāt, or, in other words, virtues and vices. No trait is considered neutral. Ghazālī, who made this classification popular, is careful to distinguish between observable behaviour and traits of character. He defines the latter as the inner disposition which renders certain kinds of behavior spontaneous and effortless and other kinds difficult and laborious. Generosity, for instance, may be inwardly present but fail to manifest itself outwardly because of the lack of means or other external obstacles, whereas a man who is not generous by nature may nevertheless choose to act generously for motives such as ambition for social eminence.

Ghazālī also states that there are four basic virtues that are the synthesis of all others: wisdom, courage, continence and balance. According to this perspective, these are defined as follows. Wisdom is the ability to distinguish right from wrong in every situation. Courage is the ability to control the self-preservation instinct. Continence is the ability to control physical appetites. Balance is the ability to use the previous abilities to keep to the middle road and avoid disequilibrium in either direction, for the self-preservation instinct if unrestrained becomes aggression, and if overly suppressed gives way to defenselessness. Similarly, there is evident harm in both suppressing physical appetites and allowing them free rein.

We shall reframe this traditional Islamic knowledge, as expounded by Ghazālī and others, to suit the contemporary mind, and, basing ourselves on the *ḥadīth*, 'I was sent to perfect nobility of character'[115] we shall adopt a perspective whereby nobility shall be considered the synthesis of all virtue. Noble is synonymous with lofty, and thus nobility by definition excludes all base or even merely petty traits, i.e., all narrowly egocentric tendencies, and includes all lofty and thus theocentric tendencies. It is possible to conceive of it as including three basic virtues which in turn include all others,

115. Aḥmad, 2/281; Mālik, *Muwaṭṭa'*, KITĀB ḤUSN AL-KHULUQ, 8.

namely: dignity, generosity and courage.

The dignity of a Muslim has its roots, as do all other virtues, in his *tawḥīd*, and is the consequence of his seeing all created beings as within the palm of their Creator, and of clearly perceiving in them the signs of His presence and power. Awareness of this awesome presence inevitably creates respect for all creatures, including oneself. It makes one humble but never servile, gentle but never weak. 'God is gentle,' says the *ḥadīth*, 'and He loves gentleness.'[116] It make one feel independent of others and well protected, but because he is aware of his own powerlessness and that of others, the dignity of a believer never turns to pride. To the extent that his faith and certainty are firm, he is safe from the vices rooted in pride such as conceit, presumptuousness, affectation and ostentation. 'The man whose heart harbors an atom's weight of pride never enters the Garden,'[117] says the *ḥadīth*, which then goes on to define pride. 'The man who admires himself and disdains others is proud.' Dignity imposes upon men restraint of their tongues and therefore forbids them stooping so low as to lie, slander, backbite, spread rumors, create scandal, or use obscenity. 'He who believes in God and the Last Day should speak in a noble manner or else remain silent.'[118] also contains modesty since, 'Modesty and faith are close companions: should one of them be lost, the other will be too.'[119] Modesty means to attire oneself decently, behave with propriety toward the opposite sex, and maintain courteous behavior at all times. It is also to refrain from eavesdropping, spying and meddling in other people's affairs. 'It is part of the soundness of a man's faith that he leaves alone that

116. Bukhārī, KITĀB AL-ADAB, 35; Muslim, KITĀB AL-BIRR, 77.

117. Muslim, KITĀB AL-IMĀN, 147.

118. Bukhārī, KITĀB AL-RIQĀQ, 23, and KITĀB AL-ADAB, 31.

119. Bukhārī, KITĀB AL-ADAB, 77; Muslim, KITĀB AL-IMĀN, 57.

which does not concern him.'[120] Finally, it is also continence (*ʿiffa*), which is both chastity and frugality. Chastity for a Muslim means confining his sexual instinct to its legally sanctioned channels, but not total abstinence, since, 'There is no monasticism in Islam.' It is to exercise self-control in accordance with *Sharīʿa* and reason, but not to attempt to suppress a natural instinct altogether. Frugality is to take from the world no more than is reasonably necessary.

> It is enough for the Son of Adam to eat a few morsels to keep his back straight; but if he must, then let him assign one third [of his stomach] to his food, one third to his beverage, and one third to his breath. Never does the Son of Adam fill a worse vessel than his stomach.[121]

Quite apart from the obvious health benefits to be gained from following such advice, simply to be in control enough to refrain from gorging oneself whenever the opportunity presents itself is a basic requirement of human dignity.

The second constituent element of nobility is generosity. It is rooted in gratitude for the uninterrupted flow of graces and favors from the Divine treasury and implies a minimum amount of detachment from the lures of the world in both their physical and social forms. It is the expansive counterpart of egocentricity. On the material plane it is to give freely and liberally for no worldly gain, to prefer others to oneself and yet still consider oneself in God's debt. The Companion, Jābir ibn ʿAbd Allāh, may God be pleased with him, once said, 'Never was the Prophet asked for anything and said, "No!"' Generosity is to give freely of one's emotions and show compassion to all created beings. 'Have compassion for those on earth and the One in heaven will have compassion on you.'[122] It is to forgive all personal offenses and refrain from thinking ill of others or

120. Tirmidhī, KITĀB AL-ZUHD, 11; Ibn Māja, KITĀB AL-FITAN, 12.

121. Tirmidhī, KITĀB AL-ZUHD, 42; Ibn Māja, KITĀB AL-AṬʿIMA, 50.

122. Tirmidhī, KITĀB AL-BIRR, 16.

exposing their weaknesses and shortcomings. Scholars have always stressed the importance of thinking-well of God and of people, as well as the dangers of thinking-ill of God and of people. Thinking well of God is to think that He keeps His promises, provides for all His creatures, and responds when called. Thinking well of people is never to attribute to a base motive an act which can at the very least be reasonably attributed to a neutral motive. It does not mean, contrary to what many people seem to think, that one should allow oneself to be fooled, even though it is better to be fooled than to think ill of someone and then turn out to be wrong. This is a delicate matter, which is generally neglected even though it is vital to the wholesomeness of one's faith.

The last constituent is courage, or the regulation of the instinct of self-preservation, which lies midway between recklessness and cowardice and, as stated before, between lack of control and aggression on the one hand and lack of assertiveness and vulnerability on the other. Physical courage is required in war and other dangerous situations. Moral courage is to speak the truth even when bitter, to be a witness for the truth even against oneself or one's kin, and to enjoin good and forbid evil against opposition.

> Upholding the truth for the truth leads to righteousness and righteousness leads to the Garden. A man will speak the truth and uphold it until he becomes established in God's sight as truthful (*ṣiddīq*). And beware of lying, for lying leads to corruption and corruption leads to the fire. A servant will lie and persist in lying until he becomes established in the sight of God as a liar.[123]

Finally, spiritual courage is to wage war against one's egotism and to resist one's appetites. The virtues, as we have mentioned, are dependent upon revealed knowledge. They may exist, albeit in an unidimensional manner in disbelievers, many of whom are by nature reasonably generous, truthful and compassionate. The

---

123. Bukhārī, KITĀB AL-ADAB, 69.

satisfaction they derive from such things, however, is entirely centered on the ego, as they are totally cut off from the vertical or spiritual dimension. But in the Muslim, the perfection of such virtues is related to the perfection of faith. The Prophet ﷺ said, 'The believer whose faith is most perfect is he whose character is most perfect.'[124] The driving force that turns knowledge into noble traits is sincerity. The absence of sincerity is the basis of vice. Sincerity, when profound enough, may lead to the conversion of a vice into its opposite virtue, or, if less profound, to acknowledging and neutralizing its more harmful effects.

Sincerity in *tawḥīd* is the unification of all of one's faculties in a single pursuit: the attainment of the good pleasure of one's Lord. It is the conformity of one's reason, imagination, emotions, impulses and physical abilities to the dictates of the highest knowledge in one's mind, which is *Lā ilāha illa'llāh*. For Divine unity implies that God demands of men all that they are, and the degree of one's sincerity is the degree to which he conforms to this demand. Thus, to attend to one's physical or emotional needs in other than the ways He has ordained or in forgetfulness of Him Who has created the needs in you is to have inner idols in the heart, each of which shares with Him the attention that should be exclusively His: *Have you seen those who have taken their passion for a god?* (25:43) These inner idols obstruct one's spiritual progress and are nefarious to the extent that one is unaware of them and is thus totally at their mercy. There is a *ḥadīth qudsī* in which God states that He brooks no associates, so that when a man shares his heart between his Lord and his passions, God abandons him to these inner idols. But if he is aware of them and struggles to free his heart so as to make it suitable to become the 'Throne of the all-Merciful,' then he eventually reaches the point where all his faculties are indeed unified in that

124. Abū Dāwūd, KITĀB AL-SUNNA, 10.

pursuit, and this is the *tawḥīd* of the heart, or true sincerity. This is why the highest expression of Divine unity in the Qur'ān was called Sūra al-Ikhlāṣ, not Sūra al-Tawḥīd, *ikhlāṣ* being sincerity. It is important to dispel any misgivings at this point by declaring that this kind of inward idolatry does not impugn one's outward declaration of *tawḥīd*, nor does it exclude one from being a Muslim as outward idolatry would immediately do. It means, however, that there is a lack of sincerity.

Lack of sincerity allows vices to appear in Muslims. The Prophet ﷺ once asked his Companions,

> 'Do you know who the destitute are?' They replied, 'The destitute among us are those who have neither money nor possessions.' He said, 'The destitute of my nation are those who arrive on the Day of Rising with their ritual prayers, *zakāt*[125] and fasts, having, however, insulted someone, slandered another, taken another's money, spilt another's blood, and beaten yet another. One will be given of their good deeds, then another, and when their good deeds are exhausted and they remain in debt, then their [victims'] sins will be taken and cast upon them, whereupon they will be thrown into the fire.'[126]

Total absence of sincerity is equivalent to disbelief or, in those who outwardly profess to be Muslims, to hypocrisy. The signs of a hypocrite are stated in *ḥadīth*, 'when he speaks he lies, when he makes a promise he does not keep it, and when he is trusted he betrays.'[127] All these are modes of treachery. The *ḥadīth* does not imply that a hypocrite will behave this way every single time, but that such behavior is for him a more frequent occurrence than its opposite.

---

125. Muslims must pay the prescribed form of charity, which is one fortieth of their savings, crops, or commerce. This is one of the five pillars of Islam and is called *zakāt*, meaning purification.

126. Muslim, KITĀB AL-BIRR, 60.

127. Bukhārī, KITĀB AL-IMĀN, 34, and KITĀB AL-ADAB, 69; Muslim, KITĀB AL-IMĀN, 107.

SOCIAL VALUES

(A) General Rules

The Qur'ān and the Sunna offer a comprehensive frame of reference which leaves out nothing that concerns both the internal and the external affairs of the Muslim community. The principles regulating every kind of social transaction were laid down along with the attitudes to adopt towards non-Muslim minorities within Muslim states. The main foundation on which all this rests is that, since all created beings are part of the one dominion belonging to the One God, they should all be shown respect, justice and compassion, with the awareness that one is dealing with Him in every transaction, not simply with the creature in question. It is legitimate to detest disbelief or vice in other men, but never to detest them as men, since they are all Adamic and have all received the Divine insufflation of the spirit which is their specific dignity. Therefore, all forms of discrimination are prohibited, let alone persecution or genocide. This is concerning human beings. As for animals, they are God's creation and belong to Him. It is only by His permission that one is allowed to slaughter animals for sustenance, but only by following the rules laid down by *Sharīʿa*, thereby ensuring that it is done with compassion, dignity, and without excess.

Muslims are enjoined to live with each other as one organism for, 'The believers, in their mutual affection, compassion, and sympathy, are as a single body; when one of its organs falls ill, the rest of the body responds with fever and sleeplessness.'[128] And, 'The Muslims are as a single construction, each part of which supports the others.'[129] And, 'None of you is a believer until he desires for

128. Bukhārī, KITĀB AL-ADAB, 27; Muslim, KITĀB AL-BIRR, 66.

129. Bukhārī, KITĀB AL-ADAB, 36.

his brother that which he desires for himself.'[130] And, 'Envy not one another, bid not higher to in ate prices for one another, antagonize not one another, turn not away from one another, and be, O servants of God, brothers! The Muslim is a brother to the Muslim, he neither oppresses him nor betrays him, neither does he lie to him nor despise him. *Taqwā* (piety or the fear of God) lies here!' he repeated three times, pointing at his chest. 'It is sufficiently evil for a man to despise his brother Muslim. The whole of a Muslim is inviolable to another Muslim: his blood, property, and honor.'[131] And, 'Whosoever relieves a believer from one of the hardships of this world, God will relieve him from one of the hardships of the Day of Rising. Whosoever lightens the burden of someone in need, God will lighten his burden in this world and the next. Whosoever shields a Muslim, God will shield him in this world and the next. And God continues to aid the servant so long as the servant is aiding his brother.'[132] Other instructions concern courtesies such as the obligation to greet other Muslims with *salām* (peace), precise instructions as to whom should greet the other first, and the spirit in which it should be done. 'A believer is affable and easy to approach. There is no good in those who are neither affable nor easy to approach.[133] Roadside and marketplace manners are also specified and so is the obligation for youngsters to respect elders and for elders to be caring and solicitous toward youngsters. '[He] Is not one of us, the one who neither respects our elders nor has compassion for our young ones.'[134]

One may then move from the general to the more specific with

130. Bukhārī, KITĀB AL-IMĀN, 7; Muslim, KITĀB AL-IMĀN, 71 and 72.

131. Bukhārī, KITĀB AL-ADAB, 57; Muslim, KITĀB AL-BIRR, 23.

132. Bukhārī, KITĀB AL-MAẒĀLIM, 3; Muslim, KITĀB AL-BIRR, 58.

133. Aḥmad, 4/400 and 5/335

134. Tirmidhī, KITĀB AL-BIRR, 15, Abū Dāwūd, KITĀB AL-ADAB, 58.

instructions regulating one's behavior towards one's neighbors, relatives, parents, spouses, children and servants. Neighborliness has always been extremely important in Muslim societies, the reason being the great emphasis placed by the Prophet himself on such relationships. Gabriel has spoken to me so often about the neighbor that I thought he would [even] allow him to inherit.'[135] And, 'Let he who believes in God and the Last Day not offend his neighbor, and he who believes in God and the Last Day let him honor his guest.'[136] And, 'None of you is a believer until his neighbor is safe from his injury.'[137] Muslims are thus strongly enjoined to look after the good interests of their neighbors, protect their families and property in their absence, and refrain from spying on them or prying into their affairs. They are forbidden to build walls so high as to obstruct the wind from reaching them. They should send a share of what they bring from the market to them and should never go to sleep unless certain that none of them sleeps hungry. There are still Muslim communities where no one would dream of sitting at his table before making sure that some of the day's cooking had been sent to his neighbor.

As for relatives in general, one should strive to know as many of them as possible so as to be able to safeguard one's ties of kinship with them. 'Know your lineages,' enjoined the Prophet, may God's blessings and peace be upon him and his family, 'that you may be able to maintain your kinship bonds.'[138] For it is one of the major social obligations of a Muslim to fulfill the rights of kinship (*ṣilat al-raḥim*). These rights include inquiring constantly about them so as to be able to assist them when they are in need, financially or

---

135. Bukhārī, KITĀB AL-ADAB, 28.

136. Ibid., 31.

137. Ibid., 29.

138. Tirmidhī, KITĀB AL-BIRR, 49.

otherwise, and preferably without their having to ask. They also include visiting them, showing them affection, and caring for the sick, the elderly, the widows and the orphans among them. When such rights are fulfilled effectively, as they were until very recently, it obviates the need for old peoples' homes, orphanages, social security systems, and all other kinds of institutions whereby the impersonal state takes over and assigns to employees the responsibilities that should normally have been incumbent upon relatives. No Muslim society should ever allow these developments to occur, for this would be yet another serious sign that faith had weakened to the point of being threatened with extinction. 'The breaker of kinship bonds does not enter the Garden,'[139] said the Prophet, may God's blessings and peace be upon him. He also said, 'Those who wish their lives to be prolonged, their provision to be increased, and to be protected against an evil death, let them fear God and safeguard their kinship bonds.'[140] And, 'The one who safeguards [his kinship bonds] is not the one who repays in kind, but the one who, when his kinship bonds are ruptured, he rejoins them.'[141]

(B) Parenthood

The Islamic definition of a woman's role is unequivocal: she is given unsurpassable superiority as a mother and placed in relative subordination as a wife. When one of the Companions asked the Prophet, may God's blessings and peace be on him, who had the most rights over him, he replied, 'Your mother.' The question was repeated twice more and twice more the same answer was given. Only on the fourth time did he say, 'Your father.'[142] Another Companion who wished to join a military expedition and

139. Muslim, KITĀB AL-BIRR, 18-19.

140. Bukhārī, KITĀB AL-ADAB, 12.

141. Ibid., 15.

142. Bukhārī, KITĀB AL-ADAB, 2; Muslim, KITĀB AL-BIRR, 1.

was seeking permission was asked, 'Do you have a mother?' The Companion replied affirmatively and was told, 'Stay with her, for the Garden is beneath her feet.'[143] And that was despite the fact that few acts in Islam rank above *Jihād*. Many other *ḥadīth*s confirm this as a general principle. This makes devotion to one's mother a direct route to Paradise. Ibn Masʿūd once asked the Prophet ﷺ about which were the best of works. He was answered that it was to perform each ritual prayer on time. 'Then which, O Messenger of God?' he asked. 'To be good to your two parents,' he replied. 'Then which, O Messenger of God?' he asked again. 'To struggle in the way of God,' was the answer.[144] This is the reverse of the Western practice of putting one's wife first, and means that in practice the usual conflicts between the mother and her daughter-in-law should always be resolved in the mother's favor, however unjust this may appear at first sight. The normal familial home used to include, until recent urbanization, all the male offspring and their families. The mother was the undisputed queen of the household and everyone lived under her wings. This relieved her of the need to compete with her daughters-in-law, and she felt secure enough to treat them well. Her powers were tyrannical but everyone knew their places and roles and it was thus rendered easy for her to be benign and motherly, and reasonable harmony was likely to reign. Her powers, however, did not extend so far as to allow her to persecute anyone in the household, force any of her sons to deprive his wife of her rights or property or mistreat or divorce her, for here the father was likely to intervene.

The father, despite his acknowledged position as head of the family, comes first only as far as his wife is concerned, but second as far as his children are concerned. Whenever the Qur'ān speaks of

143. Al-Ḥakim, *al-Mustadrak*, 4/151; Bayhaqī, *Shuʿab al-Imān*, 6/178.

144. Bukhārī, KITĀB AL-ADAB, 1.

filial duties it is to both parents that reference is made, never to the father alone, *Your Lord has decreed that you shall worship none other than Him and that you shall treat your parents graciously...* (17:23). *Thank Me and your two parents* (31:14). Thus gratitude to God should be associated with gratitude to both parents and obedience to God with obedience to the parents. Says the *ḥadīth*, 'The satisfaction of the Lord lies in the satisfaction of the parents, and His displeasure in their displeasure.'[145] And, 'God has forbidden to you to rebel against your mothers.'[146] The exception to the rule is if either parent wishes one to do something that is forbidden by *Sharīʿa*, since, 'There is no obligation to obey a created being in disobedience to the Creator.'[147] Total commitment from children toward their parents is stressed in numerous *ḥadīth*s. The Prophet said to one Companion who, having married, stopped giving financial support to his elderly father, 'You and what you possess belong to your father.'[148]

The claims of parents on their children do not stop at their deaths, for their graves should be visited regularly and they should be prayed for and offered recitations of Qur'ān. Charity should be given on their behalf, ḥajj, and ʿUmra should also be performed on their behalf whenever possible, and the people that they loved should be visited and shown all the courtesy and affection due to the memory of the departed parent. All this is very far removed from the kind of indifference that Westerners call 'autonomy,' which ranks highly in their system of values.

As for the children's claims on their parents, they should provide for them their material needs to the best of their abilities and

145. Tirmidhī, KITĀB AL-BIRR, 3.

146. Tirmidhī, 4/259.

147. Bukhārī, KITĀB AL-ADAB, 6.

148. Aḥmad, 2/179.

to the standards of their social stratum, and they should also satiate them emotionally so that they grow up secure and confident. Education and discipline come next. 'It is the child's right upon his father that he discipline him well and name him well,'[149] says one *ḥadīth*, while another states, 'For one of you to educate his son is better than to give half a measure [of grain] to the poor every day.'[150] Parents should also find their children suitable spouses when the time comes and be of good counsel to them from then on. Finally, parents should make it easy for their children to fulfill their obligations toward them, and they should avoid being too awkward or demanding.

(C) Marriage

Marriage is one of the pivotal institutions in Islam and therefore one of the most explicitly regulated. Young men are strongly enjoined to marry as early as possible, as a safeguard against irregular and therefore socially disruptive relationships, and also to enable themselves to reach maturity and stability early in their lives. It is stated in *ḥadīth* that, 'When the servant marries he completes half of his religion, let him thereafter fear God in the remaining half.'[151] Another well known *ḥadīth* explains how one should choose his spouse-to-be by stating that there are four reasons why a woman is desired for marriage: wealth, social status, beauty, and piety. The *ḥadīth* then goes on to exhort men to give piety priority over all other reasons,[152] since a pious wife is an effective helper on the road to the hereafter, whereas a worldly one is at best a distraction and at

149. Al-Haytamī, *Majmaᶜ al-Zawā'id*, 8/47; Bayhaqī, *Sunan*, 10/15; Ibn Abī Shayba, *Musannaf*, 5/219.

150. Tirmidhī, KITĀB AL-BIRR, 33.

151. Al-Ḥakim, *al-Mustadrak*, 2/161; Ṭabarānī, *Awsaṭ*, 1/294; Bayhaqī, *Shuᶜab al-Imān*, 3/383.

152. Bukhārī, KITĀB AL-NIKĀḤ, 15.

worst an actively nefarious influence. She may, for instance, put her husband under constant pressure to provide her with luxuries he can ill afford, thereby driving him to fall into dishonest acts such as embezzlement or bribery. It is in this sense that the Qur'ān warns: *O believers! Verily some of your wives and your children are your enemies, therefore beware of them!* (64:14)

The basis of the marital relationship in Islam is never passion or infatuation nor mere sexual attraction, but the kind of stable affection that makes for emotional security and thus peace and durability. The Qur'ān states: *It is He who created you out of one living soul and made of him his spouse, that he might find peace in her* (7:189). And again: *And of His signs is that He created for you, of yourselves, spouses, that you might find peace in them, and He has set between you affection and compassion* (30:21). To achieve this, rules were prescribed in *Sharīʿa* based upon the very nature of men and women and designed to make the relationship as satisfactory and stable as possible. Thus the position of each partner vis-a-vis the other and the children is unequivocally stated. Men are in charge of women, states the Qur'ān, *for that with which God has favored one of them over the other, and for that which they have expended of their wealth*...(4:34).

That which men were favored with is what allows them to carry out their functions and fulfil their responsibilities, namely an intelligence which is more objective and less subject to emotional influences, the physical strength to work outdoors, the earning power that goes with these two attributes, the responsibility to give the children their name and the consequent hereditary rights. This makes the man the main factor of stability in the household, the pivot around which all else revolves. He is therefore expected to provide material security to the best of his ability, which includes providing the household with all the necessities of life, protecting its members against external aggression, and acting as arbiter in the event of internal discord.

He should also provide emotional security and support by being a source of warmth and affection, by showing his appreciation for the effort expended within the household, and by providing sexual fulfillment. These are his this worldly duties. His religious duties are to teach his family the basics of their faith and the way to perform their acts of worship correctly, and then to supervise their implementation. He is expected to be fairly intransigent as concerns the rights of God on his family and extremely lenient as concerns his own personal rights, and never the reverse. Men should know that they will be asked to account for the way they have fulfilled these duties, for the Prophet has said, 'You are all guardians, and each of you shall be asked to account for his subjects.'[153]

Having discussed the Islamic conception of men's nature and roles let us now see what it has to say about women. The *ḥadīth* says, 'I bid you treat your women well, for women were created from a rib, the part of it that is most bent is its head, should you attempt to straighten it you will break it, and if you leave it be, it will remain bent.'[154] The *ḥadīth* obviously refers to the symbolism of the story of Eve's creation from Adam's rib. That she was created from him indicates that their natures are similar in many respects and that where they differ they are not in opposition but complement each other. The curve of the rib suggests the mother's protective and nourishing holding of her child to her breast. This is the maximum emotional output in human terms. The emotional charge required by women to function in the role of mother necessarily influences their ability to think detachedly and objectively, especially when their interests or those of their children are at stake. This is

153. Bukhārī, KITĀB AL-AḤKĀM, 1; Muslim, KITĀB AL-IMRA'A, 30.

154. Bukhārī, KITĀB AL-ANBIYĀ', 1; Muslim, KITĀB AL-RIḌĀ, 62.

why the upper end or head of the rib is said to be the part that suffers the most bending, that is, the part that is most subject to the sway of emotions. To attempt to straighten it is to attempt to force women to act like men, which, if at all possible, would forthwith deprive them of their ability to care for their children adequately. It is, however, plainly impossible, and this is why it was said in the *ḥadīth* that it would break the rib, that is, lead to the disruption of the relationship and divorce. This in no way means that there are no women who think more objectively than most men, nor that there are no men who are more emotional than most women. But it does mean that these differences should be seen in a positive not a negative light, since the fact that each provides the things that the other lacks makes for a differentiation of roles within the relationship and thus for stability. Women are required to be reasonably obedient, well groomed, efficient in the management of the household, solicitous for the children's welfare, and loyal, that is, discrete as concerns her husband's affairs and their mutual relationship.

That people are not angels and that marriage can be very difficult is an acknowledged fact in Islam, and there are therefore instructions for both parties to pre-empt or remedy the main causes of discord. The importance of safeguarding the marital relationship was very much emphasized by the fact that the Prophet ﷺ spoke of it on two of the most meaningful occasions, the Farewell Pilgrimage and on his deathbed, when he was expected to mention only matters of the utmost importance. On both occasions he bade men treat their women well and he put the onus of preserving the relationship squarely on their shoulders. He had already said, 'The best among you are those who are the best with their wives, and I am the best of you with my wives.'[155] And, 'The believer whose faith is the most perfect is he whose character is the best; and the best among you are

155. Bukhārī, KITĀB AL-NIKĀḤ, 43, and KITĀB AL-ADAB, 38.

those who are the best with their wives.'[156] He had also addressed both partners thus: 'You are all guardians and responsible for those in your charge. The ruler is a guardian, the man is a guardian over the members of his household, the woman is a guardian over her husband's house and children. You are all guardians and responsible for those in your charge.'[157]

Women are emphatically advised against one of the most common pitfalls, which is to deny their husbands' positive aspects and stress only their negative ones. They are also told that simply to perform their minimal religious obligations and to obey their husbands will guarantee them Paradise. To prevent men from taking these instructions too literally and demanding from their wives total obedience, which is recognized, in fact, to be nearly impossible, the Prophet made it clear that divorce was not to be considered lightly, since it is, 'the permitted thing that is most hateful to God.'[158] It is to be the very last resort, after all attempts at reconciliation have failed, including arbitration by the two families' elders: *And if you fear a breach between them, bring forth an arbiter from his people and an arbiter from her people; if they desire to set things right God will compose their differences* (4:35). Discretion is strongly enjoined on both spouses for obvious reasons. *Righteous women are obedient, guarding in secret that which God has guarded* (4:34) says the Qur'ān, and 'One of the worst people on the Day of Rising is a man who sleeps with his wife then one of them divulges their secret,'[159] says the *ḥadīth*.

As concerns polygamy, quite apart from such obvious advantages as, for instance, being able to have children from a second

156. Ibn Māja, KITĀB AL-NIKĀḤ, 50.

157. Bukhārī, KITĀB AL-AḤKĀM, 1; Muslim, KITĀB AL-IMRA'A, 30.

158. Abū Dāwūd, KITĀB AL-ṬALĀQ, 3.

159. Muslim, KITĀB AL-ṬALĀQ, 13 and 14; Abū Dāwūd, KITĀB AL-ADAB, 32.

wife without being forced to divorce a sterile first one, or being able to offer legally-sanctioned shelter to a widow or a divorcee and her children, the mere fact that a second wife or more is permitted, reduces the likelihood of women treating men as their exclusive possession as is seen so frequently in other cultures. To this we might add the fact that women in Islam keep their material assets independently and thus enjoy a kind of financial autonomy unknown in the West until after industrialization, particularly since the 1960s.

Finally, we have to turn to the sexual relationship between spouses and the way it is perceived by Muslims. First of all let us state, for the sake of those brought up in a different climate, that no feelings of guilt or shame are attached to this relationship. It is considered as natural and ordinary as eating and drinking and a legitimate right of both men and women. Its purpose is not only procreation, but also the strengthening of the marital bonds as well as the gratification of a natural appetite in the most pleasurable manner possible. It also has higher meanings concerning the union between pairs.

The Prophet ﷺ spoke of it to his Companions as he spoke to them about every other aspect of their daily lives. 'Let none of you approach his wife like an animal,' he once said, meaning that the approach should not be abrupt, 'but let there be a messenger between them.' They inquired what this messenger might be and he answered, 'The kiss and the word.'[160] The clear reference here is to intimate conversation, emotionally arousing words, and foreplay, that is, physically arousing gestures. He also said that one of the three things that indicated deficiency in a man was for him to approach his wife without preparing her and for him to lie with her and satisfy himself before she was satisfied. He also exhorted women to embellish themselves for their husbands and avoid rejecting their advances unless there be a genuine excuse. 'When a man

160. Quote ascribed to Daylamī, in Ghazālī's *Iḥyā' ʿUlūm al-Dīn*, 2/72.

invites his wife to his bed and she refuses and he spends the night angry with her, the angels curse her until daybreak.'[161] Muslim men and women who feel dissatisfied with their sexual life are therefore encouraged to seek appropriate advice without hesitation.

(D) Death

We have said earlier that death is nothing more than the passage from one dimension of existence into another, that the full awareness of what is to follow and knows that, as the *ḥadīth* states, 'The world is the prison of the believer and the Garden of the disbeliever.'[162] Those who long to meet their Lord in the perfection of the life-to-come experience the world's distractions and pleasures as so many obstacles standing between them and their goal. They struggle against their egos and feel their brothers' sufferings as acutely as they feel their own. They are constantly resisting the downward pull of the world and are offended and aggrieved by deviant behavior in others. They also know that, 'Those who love to meet God, God loves to meet them,'[163] and they know of the peace and delights of the Garden and the beatific vision of the Divine countenance.

The weaker a man's faith and the greater his ignorance of these matters, the greater will be his attachment to the world and reluctance to separate from it. This is why we are strongly encouraged to remember death frequently. 'Remember often the defeater of pleasures: death,'[164] said the Prophet, may God's blessings and peace be upon him. And when asked, 'Who among believers are the most sagacious?' he replied, 'Those who remember death most often and are

161. Bukhārī, KITĀB AL-NIKĀḤ, 85; Muslim, KITĀB AL-NIKĀḤ, 120 and 21.

162. Muslim, KITĀB AL-ZUHD, 1; Tirmidhī, KITĀB AL-ZUHD, 16.

163. Muslim, KITĀB AL-DHIKR, 14 and 18; Tirmidhī KITĀB AL-ZUHD, 6, and KITĀB AL-JANĀ'IZ, 67.

164. Tirmidhī, KITĀB AL-ZUHD, 4; Nasā'ī, KITĀB AL-JANĀ'IZ, 33.

the best in preparing for what follows it; those are sagacious.'[165]

He encouraged regular visits to the cemetery for the same reason. The remembrance of death detaches one from the world, reducing everything in it to its proper proportions and renders death and the events that are to follow it familiar and much less frightening. This makes death itself that much easier. Most Muslims nowadays, however, are ignorant of these things and are thus horrified by the mere mention of death. Their attitude is thus the exact opposite of what it ought to be; they come that much closer to the disbelievers' stance, who, because they know of no Paradise apart from this life, are exceedingly reluctant to leave it and can never understand that someone in his right mind should be eager to do so.

One of the obvious mercies that God bestows upon his nation is that many of those Muslims who live in forgetfulness of their lives to come are made to suffer a long illness before their death. The result is that detachment from the world and meditation on the hereafter is gradually forced on them so that when the time comes they are thoroughly prepared. This is why the notion of euthanasia does not arise in a Muslim climate. Some of the Westerners' current attitude that life must be prolonged at any cost has crept in, however, especially among Muslim medical practitioners, and by the same token the Islamic concern in providing the Muslim with a dignified death has weakened. To insist on saving someone's life at all costs may mean in many instances keeping him in intensive care with tubes coming out of every single orifice, unable to speak or say the *shahāda*,[166] and distracted by the frantic activities of the staff. It is much more important to allow a Muslim to die as he should than

---

165. Ibn Māja, KITĀB AL-ZUHD, 31.

166. The *shahāda* is the attestation of faith by which one either accepts Islam or reaffirms his adherence to it. It is to say *Lā ilāha illa'lāh*, there is no God other than God!

to try to save his life at the cost of robbing him of the opportunity to do so. For dying should be attended by godly people who will remind him to say *Lā ilāha illa'llāh* by simply repeating it in his ear, not by commanding him to say it. They should also recite Yā Sīn and other portions of the Qur'ān and continuously pray for him. The dying should be helped to remain in a state of ritual purity and to repeat their *wuḍū'*[167] whenever broken, and they should be reminded of the immensity of God's mercy, of the expected intercession by the Prophet ﷺ, and of other hopeful things. In this way the dying person may die hoping for God's mercy and expecting His forgiveness, for God says in the *ḥadīth qudsī*, 'I am as My servant thinks Me to be.'[168]

As for the family of the deceased, they should be attended to by comforting them and assisting them through their mourning. The expression of sorrow, pain and anger is encouraged and accepted, providing it does not turn into histrionics, which are strictly forbidden. They are allowed to weep and mourn to the full, but never to slap their faces or rend their clothes, although it obviously happens at times. They are reminded that, 'God is more Compassionate to them than a mother is to her infant,'[169] that this is another trial that they must suffer, and that if they would only allow Him, God will help them and put fortitude in their hearts, forgive their sins and raise their degrees for it. They are reminded that no loss equals that of the Prophet ﷺ and that even he had to suffer the death of all his children but one (Fāṭima, may Allah be pleased with her) and

167. *Wuḍū'* is ritual purification or ablution in preparation for the ritual prayer. The root of the word means 'light' and the implication of that is the indication to perform one's ablutions with purification in mind to remove some of the darkness of sin and distraction in preparation for the reception of the lights of acts of worship

168. Bukhārī, KITĀB AL-TAWḤĪD, 15 and 35; Muslim, KITĀB AL-DHIKR, 2 and 19.

169. Ibn Māja, KITĀB AL-ZUHD, 3.

of many of his loved ones. All those who come to offer their condolences are expected to participate in this assuaging process, each in his own manner. The neighbors and relatives are expected to take over the task of preparing food for the visitors, seeing to the household needs, and remaining alert for any kind of practical help that may be required of them at any time. The family will be encouraged to visit the tomb, give away charity on behalf of the deceased, pray for him, recite the Qur'ān, and, if required, perform ḥajj and ʿUmra on his behalf.

Until recently people of both sexes were encouraged to remarry not very long after losing their spouse. This resulted in the effective reorganization of their lives, materially and emotionally, and the adequate fulfillment of the children's needs.

Anger and resentment against heaven and the possibility of psychological dysfunction are again more likely to occur the more remote the bereaved person's cognitive structure is from the Islamic values and principles outlined earlier. Obviously such people will need more intensive attention.

(E) Work Ethics

Muslims are not obsessed with productivity,[170] or at least have

170. Obsession with productivity is part of the deceitful rationale of the consumer society. One author who was aware of this wrote that he wished to draw attention to, '...the invasion of human affairs by an ideology which makes deliberate use of one kind of rationality to the exclusion of all others.' Further on he talks of 'Rational Economics which prizes productivity, achieved through ever increasing efficiency, effectiveness and economy, to the exclusion of every other consideration.' He goes on to say, 'The dehumanization of work and the increasing requirement for people to fit the demands of machines became a societal norm...workers were learning to become more robot like....' He also very accurately remarks that, 'The Holy Grail being sought was the one best way to deal with people to make them produce more for as little as possible. Of course, the one best way is probably through fear but that may not be thought quite ethical unless it can be concealed by some sort of rationalization. Rationalization has been achieved by convincing people that the overriding importance of 'the bottom line' of the balance sheet is axiomatic.

not been until recently when they began to adopt blindly whatever came to them from the West. Those still aware of their traditional hierarchy of values will never measure their earthly life solely in terms of material possessions and physical pleasures. They will then work because they are required to provide for themselves and their dependents, not because there is something good in work per se, as some modern thinkers would have us believe. The only positive aspect of work these days, apart from the above stated obligation, is that it keeps many people out of mischief who might otherwise be likely to fall prey to one or more of the vices of the times. In better times, when people knew how to use their time more constructively, this did not apply.

Seen in this light, work should be kept within its proper limits and never be allowed to interfere with other duties such as acts of worship, the pursuit of religious knowledge, the nurturing of kinship bonds and other social obligations, as well as recreational activities within lawful limits. Those unable to earn are the direct responsibility of their nearest relatives, and it is extremely dishonorable to allow them to be cared for in an institution.

It is incumbent on every Muslim to make himself as useful as possible to his community, not only by his formal contribution to the economy or the benefits derived from his job as such, but in all the ways demonstrated by the Sunna, such as by learning and teaching others what he has learned, offering good counsel and emotional support to those who need them, and so on. These aspects of a Muslim's responsibilities are coming to be neglected with increasing urbanization and alienation; the only activity nowadays granted the honorable label of 'useful' is work.

The situation has been attacked by Critical theorists who highlight the selective use of reason to bolster particular vested interests against social justice.' See C. Baldwin, Psychiatric Bulletin, 1996, 530-31.

Whatever has to be done should always be done with efficiency and precision. 'God has decreed that everything you do should be done with excellence,'[171] says the *ḥadīth*. A Muslim is thus obliged to keep his activities under constant scrutiny and never allow himself to fall short of the required standard or be guilty of neglect. The extent to which he fails to comply with this rule is the degree to which his faith and knowledge of the requirements of his religion are defective. A Muslim strives for excellence in every act in the awareness that it is God who is watching him, not his foreman. The extent to which Muslim societies are failing to function efficiently is a result of the weakness that has befallen their faith and that has become ubiquitous.

It has become clear beyond dispute that modern technology, production lines and bureaucracy dehumanize people. Nothing can be done about this at the moment except to try to counteract these effects by deliberate and intensive religious and cultural input in the workers' free time.

As for women, Islam allows them to go out to work in case of necessity; in other words, there has to be a justification valid enough for a woman to leave her territory, which is the home, and venture out in the jungle. Previously a woman's education consisted in the knowledge and discipline necessary for her specific functions and for her life-to-come. The latter gave her a dimension of profundity Muslim, and far-sightedness. In today's urban communities most women receive a technical education that raises their expectations and allows them no peace of mind if they stay at home. At the same time, religious education is totally neglected even in 'cultured' individuals. This state of affairs renders it psychologically necessary for them to go out to work, and we must accept and adapt to this necessity, with the reservation, however, that this does not impinge

171. *Kitāb al-Sayd*, 57.

on their primary responsibilities, which concern the family. Islam always stresses the importance of practical solutions and to claim, as only fanatics do, that it denies women the right to work, leaving them chronically dissatisfied, is nonsensical.

6. ISLAMIC PSYCHOTHERAPY

Effecting changes in one's environment by means of verbal and non-verbal communication is a constant human activity. More specifically, to effect psychological changes in another person is the aim of all human communication. This aim may be explicit or implicit, and the changes aimed at may be as superficial and short-term as assuaging a distressed child or eliciting laughter by telling a joke, or as long and more pervasive as training a soldier to kill or a doctor to heal. To take a young man with ordinary emotional responses and attitudes and turn him into a disciplined, blindly obedient person, ready to maim or kill another without hesitation, is to effect a profound psychological change indeed. Doctors, bank clerks, and policemen, all have to deal with the general public; however, the training processes of each group aims for a different set of attitudes and responses. All these changes are effected by means of various combinations of cognitive and behavioral maneuvers that mankind has known about and practiced for thousands of years. Out of this vast range of activities, psychotherapy, or the treatment of psychological dysfunction, occupies an extremely narrow domain.

In Muslim societies, the area which corresponds to the current definition of psychotherapy was an integral part of a larger area involving most of the learned and wise men in the community and aiming at reducing the distance between people and the norm as defined earlier, i.e., a model based on the Sunna. Remoteness and deviation from this model was seen to be what properly constituted abnormality and required correction. Clearly, such abnormality would be of many different modes and degrees, and only at the outer fringes of this range do we find what is today considered as pathological. Madness, that is schizophrenia, manic-depressive disorders and organic psychoses belong to an altogether different domain: they are regarded as illnesses requiring medical attention, and are considered by *Sharīʿa* to relieve those who suffer from them from their religious obligations, since the prerequisite of obligation is sanity.

Prevention has always been considered much more important than cure in traditional societies. A good example is that of China, where the occurrence of illness used to be considered a failure by the physician to carry out proper prevention. Instead of receiving payment from his clients, which he did as long as they remain healthy, once they fell ill he had to pay them! In psychosocial terms, prevention amounts to inculcating the set of attitudes most likely to render people immune to breakdown in case of excessive stress and more likely to carry out their social functions in a healthy manner. In Islamic terms this means helping them to assimilate and put into practice the concepts outlined in this book. People always resorted to the learned in the community for advice in times of crisis, for this was the natural thing to do and they did it long before the stress built up to the extent of affecting them adversely. When the crisis escalated, the same men were required to intervene and make peace among families or between spouses. They provided counseling in all kinds of matters including sexual problems, had family sessions similar to what we would call family therapy today, knew about grief and grief work and also about prescribing medicinal herbs. For the majority of them the question of fees never even arose because they worked simply to discharge what they viewed as part of their religious duty to the community. Such sages are becoming rarer by the day, especially in the urbanized areas, and their tasks are now being handed over, Western style, to professionals.

These professionals share with their predecessors the things that are now known to be common to all psychotherapies,[172] but they differ from them in having acquired in the course of their Western education a fragmented view of man and the universe and in having lost sight of the kind of Islamic knowledge that should have been theirs by birthright.

---

172. That there are non-specific features common to all psychotherapies and responsible for most of the positive results was suggested by Jerome Frank in 1973, and this insight has come to be generally accepted as valid. These common features include: a locale designated as a place of healing; an intense relationship with a person or group; a rationale or myth to explain the problem and the treatment, i.e. to suggest to the 'patient' that the therapist knows what he is doing; non-specific methods of boosting self-esteem; and the provision of experiences of success. Others have suggested factors, again non-specific, which were thought to affect outcome: assets the patient already has, such as being young, intelligent, articulate and successful. Factors in the therapist were suggested by Carl Rogers to include the ability to have unconditional positive regard for the client, to empathize accurately, and to be genuine or congruous. Nonspecific factors in group therapy, i.e., factors unrelated to the therapist's denomination, were suggested by Irvin Yalom to be: interpersonal learning; the opportunity for catharsis; group cohesiveness; acquiring insight into one's problems; developing socializing techniques; the instillation of hope; universality, i.e. recognizing that others suffer from similar or more severe predicaments; altruism, i.e. the opportunity to boost self-esteem by being seen to be capable of helping others, receiving guidance, and so on. What all this amounts to is that those in distress who find people with enough stability, wisdom, affection, concern, and time to help them have a good chance of overcoming their difficulties. For further details see C. R. Rogers, *Client Centered Therapy*, Houghton-Miflin, Boston, 1951; C. R. Rogers, 'The Necessary and Sufficient Conditions of Therapeutic Personality Change', Journal of Consultative Psychology, 21 (1957), 459-461; and Irvin Yalom, *The Theory and Practice of Group Psychotherapy*, Basic Books, New York, 1975 (2nd ed.).

Professionals must first of all familiarize themselves and gain reasonable proficiency in the various Islamic sciences that have a direct bearing on their work. They must truly assimilate the Islamic teachings on the structure of the universe, that of man, the Intermediary World, the various forces influencing human behavior, the ethical aspect, the normal model against which to measure human beings, and the textual evidence to be offered in the course of cognitive restructuring. They also must acquaint themselves with the popular views of psychological disorder as caused by jinn, magic, or the evil eye (*ḥasad*). These are of course real possibilities, but the common tendency is to attribute every disturbance to them rather than to the more usual intrapsychic and interpersonal stresses and disequilibria. There are numerous formulas of *dhikr* (invocations) which have a profound and often dramatic effect on correcting misconceptions and these should be known and used freely.

Can we say that there is a specifically Islamic kind of psychotherapy? The answer is both yes and no. Yes, inasmuch as any kind of intervention based on Islamic principles and using Islamic models and criteria must obviously be regarded as specifically Islamic. No, inasmuch as there will be, of necessity, many ideas and techniques that will have to be borrowed from the West. Today is professionals are much more likely to study the techniques of various kinds of therapies from Western textbooks and not from traditional Islamic sources. This is not far removed from the situation of the Muslim world in the early days of the Abbasid caliphate when the Muslims translated works on philosophy, medicine, astronomy, geography, and so on, from Greek to Arabic, evaluated them according to the revealed knowledge of the Qur'ān and *ḥadīth*, assimilated whatever they found compatible and discarded whatever they thought was not.

Islamic psychotherapy will then include various forms of counseling and supportive measures, and also cognitive and behavioral techniques. Theories such as Freud's, which contradict the Islamic perspective outright, are to be rejected wholesale. Other theories, such as those speaking of 'dysfunctional thoughts' or 'basic assumptions' and how to alter them may easily be adapted for use in an Islamic context. Almost all behavioural manoeuvres are acceptable, the exception being where the technique has something legally prohibited about it, such as the use of surrogate partners. There is nothing against the use of psychotropic drugs much in the same way as they are currently used.

Muslim psychotherapists have much to do to evaluate, accept or reject, and adapt to their own needs the scores of ideas currently in circulation in the West. This has to be done painstakingly and thoroughly and, more importantly, only after having done the necessary preparation by studying the Islamic perspective. This perspective will have to be taught at universities. There will have to be detailed expositions of the step-by-step application of each adapted idea; in other words, clear how-to manuals will have to be written for the day-to-day use of professionals in the field.

7. WAR

According to Islamic sacred law, war is considered an evil that may be resorted to only when absolutely necessary and in the most limited manner possible, the hateful exception rather than the rule in human relationships. The only thing that the Qur'ān sanctions even while describing as hateful is fighting: *Fighting has been decreed upon you and is hateful to you* (2:216). The Prophet forbade his men to exhibit eagerness in anticipation of battle, saying, 'O people, do not desire to encounter the enemy, rather ask God for safety. Should you then meet them, be steadfast and know that the Garden is under the shadow of the swords.'

Whenever fighting is mentioned in relation to Islam, the word *Jihād* inevitably comes up. There is widespread confusion concerning the meaning of *Jihād*, however; for in reality it involves much more than simply combat. There are three terms that ought to be understood in this context: *Jihād*, which means struggle or exertion, *Qitāl*, which means warfare or combat, and *Irhāb*, which means terrorism. The first two are frequently used in the Qur'ān, whereas the third was coined recently to describe violent acts against civilians. The confusion arises from using the term *Jihād* to mean all three. This is frequently done in bad faith, sometimes in ignorance, chiefly by certain orientalists and the media in the West, but also by extremist Muslim groups. The former are used to looking at other cultures and civilizations through Western binoculars and seem to be unable to understand the development and evolution of "others" except in terms of their own. One example is their inability to understand the Caliphate, which is a civil state governed by Islamic law, only in terms of a catholic theocracy and an infallible papacy, and in the light of the long history of oppression of the poorer classes in Europe that eventually led to revolutions. Therefore they have come to conceive of civil rights and liberties as possible only in the absence of religion and sacred law, and of the relationship between a believer and his Lord as strictly individual and separate from social, political, and scientific endeavors. By contrast, Islamic sacred law guarantees the rights of citizenship to every citizen, whatever his faith, leaving no room for the development of anything like anti-Semitism or the inquisition. Oppression of the poorer classes came about very late in Muslim history, when the rulers had drifted so far from their original Islamic ideals that social oppression and corruption became widespread.

What then is *Jihād*? As defined by the authoritative Arabic dictionary, *Lisān al-ᶜArab*, *Jihād* is to exert oneself to the utmost and to the limit of one's ability in action or in speech. It is thus not confined to action, let alone violent action. In Qur'ānic terms *Jihād* is to exert oneself to the utmost in calling oneself and others to God and defending one's liberty to do so. Calling oneself to God means imposing upon oneself obedience to His sacred law and striving for sincerity of the heart through the battle against the evils of one's ego. Calling others means conveying the message clearly and courteously, and enjoining good and forbidding evil. The battlefield of Islamic *Jihād* is thus seen to involve primarily the world of ideas and beliefs. According to the Qur'ān and the Sunna of the Prophet Islamic *daʿwa* should be done wisely, graciously, and engagingly: *Call to the way of your Lord with wisdom and gracious exhortation, and debate with them in the best of manners* (16:125).

Islam rejects the philosophy of struggle, the concept of the survival of the fittest, such as promoted by communism and evolutionary theory, for it leads to the physically stronger overpowering and either annihilating the weaker, or imposing his ideas, culture, and values on him, thereby ending diversity, which is an essential attribute of God's creation. Islam also rejects all philosophies that consider fighting and killing natural to human beings, instincts that are inborn in them. On the contrary, Islam regards the human race as made of potentially spiritual beings that are destined for immortality in a life to come. The fittest in Islamic terms are the Prophets and saints of God who far from wishing to exterminate or survive at the expense of the unfit, only wish to illuminate their path for them.

Muslims are enjoined always to start by calling their own selves to God before engaging in calling others. To call oneself to God is to fear Him, guard oneself against His wrath by avoiding everything that He forbids, and remember Him constantly, humbly, and sincerely, while striving to purify one's heart. He who wishes to call others to God should discipline himself adequately first, otherwise he may fall prey to the tricks of the untamed ego and end up doing more harm than good. This is the Greater *Jihād* which unfortunately is invariably ignored by extremists who seem able to perceive evil only in others, never in their own selves.

To serve one's parents graciously, show compassion and generosity to one's family, kin, neighbors, the Muslim community at large, and then the rest of humanity is *Jihād*. So is striving to bring prosperity to the land, to manage the resources of the planet responsibly, to treat human beings, animals, plants, and inanimate matter with care and compassion, thereby fulfilling one's role as God's vicegerent on earth. Had the Muslims of these times been true to their faith they would have been the first to combat global pollution with vigour.

To call others to God by exerting oneself to the utmost to acquire and disseminate knowledge, to exhort them to believe in God and lead a morally upright life, and to counsel them against disbelief and corrupt behavior, is *Jihād*.

Jihād is thus to exert oneself to the utmost and to the limits of one's capacity in many different domains, only one of which is combat. This is why *Jihād* is an obligation that is incumbent upon all Muslims, men and women, since each is required to exert himself to the best of his abilities to improve his and his community's religious, physical, social, political, and environmental status. As for combat, which is only a special from of *Jihād*, it is subject to conditions that must be fulfilled and is confined to specific situations.

To confine the meaning of *Jihād* to warfare is one error; another is to confuse between *Jihād* and a war of religious coercion. *Jihād* is often called 'holy war,' which implies that it is a war of religion specifically directed against the adherents of other religions to force Islam upon them. Such a holy war is thought to be one where everyone who is not a Muslim is an enemy. *Jihād*, however, is not a religious holy war, since Islam rejects religious coercion in all its forms and teaches that faith is a secret in the heart, between the believer and his Creator, based on understanding and conviction. It can never be the result of coercion, let alone coercion of a violent nature. This is why the Qur'ān affirms unequivocally that *there is no coercion in religion* (3:256). This verse is to be understood both as a prohibition against imposing religion by coercion and as a denial of the very possibility of bringing about true adherence to religion through coercion, for fear can only produce false pretence, never true belief. This is why there are numerous verses in the Qur'ān saying to the adversaries, *To you your religion and to me mine* (109:6). *He who so wishes let him believe and he who so wishes let him disbelieve* (18:29). While other verses define the limits of the responsibility of the Messenger: *Upon the Messenger is only to convey [the message]* (5:99). *Therefore remind, for you are but a reminder, you have no power over them* (88:21, 22). That this was clearly understood by Muslims is proved by the historical fact that there is no record of Christians, Jews, Zoroastrians, or Hindus ever being coerced into becoming Muslims. There was never anything like the inquisition in Islam.

Islam insists on the importance of preserving the freedom of the homeland, its independence, and the right, or rather the duty of each citizen to lead a free life in a free homeland. This is considered more important than life itself and was clearly stated to be so at a time when the concept of nationalism had yet to appear.

There are five things that the Islamic sacred law declares that it is expressly designed to protect. The first of these is religion, then come life, property, honor, etc... Combat is legally sanctioned only to protect these five sacrosanct things.

At the beginning, when the early Muslims surrounding the Prophet were persecuted because of their faith, expelled from their hometown, Makka, and forced to emigrate, first to Abyssinia then to Madina. God, following years of enjoining patience upon them, finally permitted them to fight back. The justification for the permission is stated to be that they were being wronged, which means persecuted and expelled from their homes:

> *Permission to fight is granted to those who are attacked because they were wronged; God is indeed able to give them victory. Those who were expelled from their homes without right, except that they say 'our Lord is God'. Had God not checked some of the people by means of others, monasteries, churches, synagogues, and mosques,*

> *wherein God's Name is much mentioned, would have been destroyed.* (22:39-41)

Once an Islamic state was established and the enemy fought to obstruct the transmission of the message and obliterate the new religion in its cradle, permission became obligation:

> *And fight in the way of God those who fight you, but do not attack them first, for God loves not the aggressors. And slay them wherever you come upon them, and expel them from where they expelled you, for persecution is worse than slaying. But fight them not in the Sacred Mosque unless they should fight you there; then if they fight you, slay them. Such is the reward of the disbelievers. But if they give over, then God is Forgiving, Compassionate. Fight them till there is no persecution and the religion becomes all God's; then if they give over then let there be no hostility save against the transgressors. The Holy Month for the Holy Month; holy things demand reciprocity. He who commits aggression against you, commit aggression against him like as he has committed against you; and fear God, and know that God is with the Godfearing.* (2:190-94)

As seen from this passage, the instructions are not to attack first, but only when attacked, to fight vigorously but respect the ban on fighting in the Sanctuary, unless the ban is broken by the enemy, and to cease hostilities immediately the enemy gives over, at which time God enjoins forgiveness and compassion. The aim as here stated is to fight until an end is put to persecution and everyone is free to believe in God if they so wish.

Once fighting breaks out, Islamic sacred law imposes upon it a set of strict moral rules. These were taught by the Prophet to his companions on various occasions as dictated by circumstances. On one of these occasions, as he was campaigning, he came upon a dead woman that had been killed by the vanguard. He exclaimed, "This woman would not have been fighting!" Then he ordered one of his companions to catch up with the leader of the vanguard and bid him to forbid his men from killing women, children, and hired workers." Anas ibn Mālik related that the Prophet used to say,

"Go in the name of God, by God, according to the religion of the Messenger of God. Do not kill a frail old man, a child, and infant, or a woman. Do not take any of the spoils by yourself, be virtuous, and act with excellence, for God love those act with excellence." Other companions related that whenever he sent an expedition he enjoined upon the leader the fear of God and to take good care of his men, then he forbade them any form of treachery, mutilation of corpses, killing children, or attacking any of the hermits and monks that used to live in the desert on the outskirts of towns in the first centuries of Christianity.

These instructions were remembered by the companions and acted upon when necessary. The instructions concerning treachery, for instance, were brought to the fore when Muʿāwiya during his caliphate moved to muster his forces on the borders of Byzantium so as to attack them immediately the truce between them expires. The Companion ʿAmr ibn ʿAbsa considered this a kind of treachery and rode up to Muʿāwiya exclaiming, "*Allāhu Akbar! Allāhu Akbar!* Loyalty, not treachery!" Then he said to him, "I have heard the Messenger of God – may God' blessings and peace be upon him – say, 'He who has made a pact with other people should neither tie a knot nor untie it until the time of the pact ends or he has given them clear notice." In that companion's opinion, the Prophet's instructions were to be interpreted as giving sufficient notice to the enemy before resuming hostility. Muʿāwiya, himself a companion, accepted this interpretation.

Abū Bakr, the Prophet's first successor, summing up the instructions given by the Prophet on several occasions, commanded the leaders of military expeditions to consider those priests who fight among the enemy forces as combatants, but not monks and hermits who were unlikely ever to fight and were thus to be left alone. Then he forbade them to kill women, children, elderly or sick people, to cut down fruitful trees, ruin anything at all that is flourishing, kill animals except for food, burn or drown palm groves, destroy wells, mutilate human beings or animals, and behave treacherously or with cowardice. These instructions are to be implemented strictly even when the enemy kills Muslim women and children and confiscates their land, homes, and other property. There is no disagreement among jurist as to any of the above, but there is disagreement as to whether it is lawful to attack enemy personnel at times when they are on leave, unarmed, and unprepared.

The decision to wage war must be taken by the appropriate authority, for legally acceptable reasons, and waged against combatants, in conformity with Islamic sacred law. Instructions are to this day be found in manuals of Islamic law. An Islamic state is at peace with those who are not at war with the Muslims, have not invaded their land, expelled them from it, or persecuted them in religion. This is what the Qur'ān states clearly when it says:

> *God forbids you not, as regards those who have not fought you in religion, nor expelled you from you homes, that you should treat them kindly and with justice, for God surely loves the just. God only forbids you as to those who have fought you in religion and expelled you from your homes, or have helped in your expulsion, that you should take them for friends. Those who do are the unjust.* (60:7-9)

God loves justice. He loves kindness and compassion even more. Therefore, the least acceptable level in dealing with non Muslims is to treat them with fairness, both in times of peace and in times of war.

As for *Irhāb*, terrorism, it is the use of violence to frighten others and coerce them into accepting that which they have no wish for. It is most often practiced by governments against their own subjects, terror by the state to subdue the citizens, or against the subjects of another country. It may also be practiced by extremist groups, communist in the past, Islamist at present, to force a certain course of action on the targeted government to submit to their demands.

The first appearance of the concept of terror was in Europe during the French revolution, when the mass executions carried out by the revolutionaries caused their time to be called the Reign of Terror. Pogroms as carried out in Europe, expelling people from their homes and turning them into refugees, and killing some to frighten the others into abandoning their lands, such as Israel's long standing war of terror against the Palestinian civilian population, is terrorism at its worst. Islam not only rejects terrorism in all its forms, but it teaches that none of the revealed religions has ever condoned terror, violence, or coercion, as means to spread their teachings or impose their sacred laws. The Qur'ān says that when God sent Moses to Pharaoh, He said to Moses, '*Speak to him gently, that perhaps he may take heed or fear [the consequences of opposing the will of God]*' (20:44). As for Christianity, it is based on turning the other cheek and total rejection of violence, an ideal betrayed consistently by the violence of Christians over the centuries.

The word *Irhāb* is used for terrorism in Arabic but has connotations different to those it has in English. The root *R-h-b*, which means fear, and its derivatives, are mostly used in the Qur'ān within the context of the fear and awe of God. A *Rāhib* is a monk or a hermit, one who is so full of the fear of God that it deters him not only from sins, but also from indulging in worldly pleasures, so that he shuns the world and devotes his life to His worship. There is an obvious link here between fear and deterrence. This link is clear in the Qur'ānic use of the word for terror such as it appears in Sūrat al-Anfāl for instance, in a passage that contains explicit instructions for the conduct of hostilities and needs to be understood according to the context, which was an actual state of war, some of the enemies were breaking their treaties, while others were lying in wait for the chance to pounce on the Muslims. There was thus a pressing need for deterrence. This is why the verses exhort the Muslims to muster sufficient forces to strike terror into the hearts of their enemies and thus deter them from carrying out their intended aggression.

> *Those of them with whom you have made a treaty, but who at every opportunity break their treaties and have no fear of God; should you vercome them in battle, then disperse those who are behind them, that perhaps they may take heed. And if you fear treachery from any people, then throw back to them [their treaty] fairly; for God loves not the treacherous. And let not those who disbelieve think that they will be able to outstrip, they cannot escape. Prepare for them what you are able to of forces and tethered horses to strike terror into God's enemies and yours, and others beside them whom you do not know, but whom God knows. Whatever you spend in the way of God will be repaid to you in full and you will not be wronged. And should they lean toward peace, lean toward it, and trust in God, for He is the Hearing, the Knowing.* (8:56-61)

The verses clearly state that if the enemy is deterred and asks for peace, the Muslims should accept it forthwith, placing their trust in God to protect them from further betrayals. The Muslims themselves are strictly forbidden treachery, for God loves not the treacherous.

Apart from those with Muslim names who have committed atrocities in the name of ideologies alien to Islam such as communism or Baathism, the Muslim war record is clean. Muslims were never accused of genocide, they never perpetrated the kinds of massacre perpetrated for instance by the crusaders who slaughtered seventy thousand people on conquering Jerusalem, so that their horses waded knee-deep in blood, by the Spanish in Spain, and in central and south America which they plundered in the name of religion, by the Italians when they massacred, starved, and gassed the Libyans in the name of civilization, by the French who even while glorifying their own resistance fighters, ruthlessly massacred Moroccan and Algerian resistance fighters, eventually resulting in a million Algerians losing their lives in their struggle for freedom. The list can go on. This is to be contrasted with the chivalrous behavior of the leaders of *Jihād* in Algeria, Libya, Chechnya, and elsewhere in Muslims lands that had once been under the oppressive rule of imperialism. These leaders were eminently pious and learned men whose chivalrous behavior remains a model that the self styled mujahidin of today would do well to study. They never repaid in kind the atrocities their enemies, but scrupulously preserved the honor of their religion and their cause.

A good recent example of how Muslims wage war is Bosnia. The Bosnian Muslims were massacred, buried in mass graves, tortured, starved in concentration camps, and their women were raped. They never retaliated in kind. None of the war criminals under trial are Muslims. The Bosnians, being a traditional Sunni, Hanafi community, knew that to behave like animals meant relinquishing the honour of belonging to the community of Muḥammad, may God's blessings and peace be upon him.

The decision to wage war and the responsibility to make sure it is justifiable rests with the government of any given Islamic nation. Small groups are not allowed to take the law into their own hands and wage their own private war. To obey the ruler even when he is weak or corrupt is explicitly stated to be preferable to causing sedition and civil unrest. To abandon obedience to the government's instructions amounts to no less than placing oneself outside the fold of Islam, again even when the government in question is not behaving according to Islamic law, for Islam seeks to avoid chaos and suffering at all cost and always prefers the lesser of any two evils. The reasoning that since most people witness their governments' inept and sometimes anti-Islamic conduct and do nothing about it they must be as guilty as they is alien to orthodox Islamic thought. It is unjustifiable for Muslims, some of them young and under the sway of emotions, to reject the views of our leading scholars and adopt a manner of thinking so dangerously in opposition to that of centuries of profound scholarship. By doing so they become renegade groups (*khawārij*). This becomes blindingly obvious when one thinks that they always end up attacking Muslim men, women, and children, the very people they claim to be fighting for. There is a clear difference between commando operations and terrorism. The former is a military operation, carried out against a military target, praiseworthy so long as the cause is just. The latter is not a military operation, its target may be the indiscriminate killing of civilians, and it can never be sanctioned by Islamic law. Wars are waged according to the agreements and treaties of the times. In our time one of those is the Geneva Convention. Muslims are bound by their faith to observe their pledges scrupulously. Finally, let us reiterate that Muslims, as chaotic as they have become, are the last bastion of revealed principles. We must never allow ourselves to forget this and be deceived by the brutality of our foes into retaliating in kind and forsaking our law. Those who know nothing about the rules of warfare should spend some time learning about them before pronouncing on this or that matter. The Prophet ﷺ has described our times and the evil in them very clearly. As shown above he has given explicit instructions as to how to cope with these situations and their problems. One cannot pretend to be a Muslim yet neglect to acquire this kind of knowledge which is his only safeguard against the deceptions and temptations of the times.

CHAPTER REFERENCES:

Bukhārī, *Ṣaḥīḥ*, *Kitāb al-Jihād wal siyar*, Bāb 112 , 156:2966, 3025, 3026; Muslim, *Ṣaḥīḥ*, Kitāb al-*Jihād*, 1742; Abū Dāwūd, *Kitāb al-Jihād*, 2613, 2614, 2631; *Lisān al-ʿArab*, 3:135; Abū Dāwūd, *Kitāb al-Jihād*, 2669; Ibn Ḥibbān, *Ṣaḥīḥ*, 4789, 4791; al-Ḥakim, *Mustadrak*, 2565; Abū Dāwūd, *Kitāb al-Jihād*, 2614; Muslim, *Ṣaḥīḥ*, *Kitāb al-Jihād*, 1731; Tirmidhī, *Kitāb al-Siyar*, Bab 48:1617; Abū Dāwūd, *Kitāb al-Jihād*, 2613; Ibn Maja, 1617; Aḥmad, Musnad, 23080; Bayhaqī, al-*Sunan al-*

Kubra, 9/89, 90; Abū Dāwūd, *Kitāb al-Jihād*, 2759; Bayhaqī, *al-Sunan al-Kubra*, 9/231; Bayhaqī, *al-Sunan al-Kubra*, 9/89, 90; Imām Mālik, *Muwaṭṭa'*, 965; ʿAbd al-Razzāq, *Musannaf*, 9375, 9376.

CONCLUSION

The approach adopted throughout this book has been to consider each topic by studying its physical, psychological, social, and spiritual parameters. Accordingly, a psychological event such as an emotion or a cognition, whether or not leading to outwardly observable behavior, may be conceived as either triggered off or influenced by one or more factors from these parameters. On the physical plane we may consider factors from the past such as heredity and learned patterns of simple behavior, as well as immediate factors such as the input from the sensory apparatus, the activation of physical appetites, and the state of health of the person in question. On the psychological plane we may again think of heredity, of past memories, of cognitive structure, of suggestions either from the higher or the lower worlds, and of virtuous and non-virtuous tendencies. Then there are the social transactions to consider, and finally the spiritual parameter proper, which is the degree of influence of the spirit on the other elements and their conformity to Revelation. Let us here again stress the fact that the word 'spiritual' must be used exclusively for things which transcend both the cognitive and emotional levels, since these belong to the psychological domain. The use of the word for everything religious, regardless of its particular level, is abusive, despite the fact that this sense is very common nowadays. It may help to clarify this point if we consider the ancient teaching that man and the universe are mirror images of each other. Imām ʿAlī, may God be pleased with him, expressed this in a verse:

You may think you are a small body
yet within you is the greater universe.

It is easy to see that man's body corresponds to the material world, his soul or psyche to the Intermediary Realm, and his heart in its higher aspect-his spirit, in other words-to the highest worlds, or the spiritual world of lights, which transcends all forms. We have already quoted the saying that, 'The heart of the believer is the Throne of the All-Merciful,' and cited the correspondence between the inward and the outward hearts. Each of these four parameters is subject to three kinds of tendencies, which are the upward pull of the higher worlds, the downward pull of the lower worlds, and the dispersing effect of the terrestrial world.

Another important principle to be noted is that for any kind of knowledge to be useful and not liable to result in major calamities it must be based on revelation. The observable information that we gather from the environment using our senses and their artificial extensions must be organized within a framework based on revealed principles, in other words, it must be controlled from above. As for the current method of gathering information and then trying to construct a theory from the bottom up, it can lead to nothing that is worth knowing. Whatever valid results are obtained by this method are likely to be gravely misused because its lack of principles based on revelation allows all kinds of suggestions to penetrate it. Suggestion in its higher sense is inspiration; in its lower sense, it is the insinuations of the Devil. Men of God elaborating on revealed texts and drawing practical conclusions differ from psychoanalysts precisely because the former are inspired from above and the latter from below. Everything in creation has its inverted image, or caricature. The similarity lies in the form and the opposition in the meaning. Both Jesus and the Impostor claim to be the Christ and both have the ability to perform supernatural deeds; their outward similarity deceives the ignorant and those with vested interests. Madness is the inverted image of spiritual ecstasy, and many psychiatrists are entirely unable to differentiate between the two. Psychoanalysts claim that the relationship between the child and his parents subsists in the grown-up child as the need to extrapolate and to apply it to the relationship between him and God. Thus they explain mankind's need for religion. This is the inverted image of the truth, since the relationship between any person and any figure of authority is nothing but the shadow or the reflection of the relationship between that person and his Lord. Authority figures are manifestations of the Divine Name al-Rabb, the Lord; 'The sovereign is the shadow of God on earth,'[173] says a *ḥadīth*. We have already discussed how everything created is but the manifestation of various combinations of Divine Names and Attributes. We must now add that the more purely the attribute is manifested, the easier it is to perceive and the closer it is to perfection at its level and vice versa. The attribute of Lordship implies sovereignty, provision, protection, solicitude, responsiveness and instruction in both worldly and other-worldly matters. The same should in principle apply to the relationship between kings and subjects, masters and servants, superiors and inferiors, and so on. However, perfection does not belong to creatures, except the highest among them, who are the Prophets, and then it is still relative, not absolute, perfection. Thus we may see, for example, sovereignty without solicitude, which is then termed tyranny,

173. Al-Haytamī, *Majmaʿ al-Zawā'id*, 2/215 and 4/134; Bayhaqī, *Shuʿab al-Imān*, 6/16 and 18.

and the same may be applied to the other attributes.

Although these concepts are vital to all Muslims, and even to non-Muslims, it is not the role of this book to develop them further here. It has not been the intention to give a full exposition of the subjects discussed, but rather to indicate as clearly and briefly as possible where the modern trend has gone wrong, why it has done so, and how to proceed in rectifying one's position on each subject, by aligning it with that which we have no doubt is entirely true, namely, revealed knowledge. Such background knowledge is necessary to anyone who intends to participate in solving conceptually and practically our current problems and who is concerned not to fall into the same kind of absurdities that the West is remorselessly pursuing. No Muslim should accept modern ideas uncritically, and no Muslim should undertake a critique based on anything other than the knowledge of the Qur'ān and Sunna. The principles that we need today or will ever need are to be found there. There and nowhere else are the foundations of our thinking and solutions to be found. I hope that by writing this book I shall have, in some small measure, done my part.

Some people are more capable of theoretical thinking, others of drawing practical conclusions from such thinking. Both talents are necessary in developing an Islamic formulation of psychology, sociology, anthropology, history, and other sciences, adequate for the requirements of the times. This book is an invitation to those possessing these talents to assess for themselves the validity of the concepts it contains and then develop them further. Much remains to be done but the task is not one that concerns professionals alone. It must be seen in the greater context of re-educating the community, including the professionals, in their lost heritage, and of formulating firm foundations for any scientific endeavor. It has become essential for everyone to be aware of these principles, for the confusion of the times is sure to escalate, and, at the current speed of events, our children or perhaps even we ourselves are very likely to be forced to choose between the Mahdī and the Dajjāl. At that point ignorance of the criteria upon which to make the choice will equal nothing less than the fire of Hell.[174]

174. Hell is remoteness from the All-Merciful. The more the distance, the thicker the veils, the less mercy penetrates, and the more opaque the shadows. The fire of Hell is black. Paradise, on the other hand, is the proximity of the All-Merciful. It is flooded with light, everything in it is luminous, the veils are transparent, and souls are immersed in the ocean of mercy. The Mahdī is a mercy from God, a man of light who guides others to the gates of Paradise, while the Impostor (*Dajjāl*), the Antichrist, is a man of darkness, a temptation from God, who lures others towards the gates of Hell. Again, revealed knowledge is light, ignorance is darkness; consequently, the first leads to Paradise, the second to Hell.

WORKS CITED

Abū Dāwūd, *Sunan*, Dār al-Kutub al-ʿIlmiyya, Beirut, 3 vols., 1996 ce.

Abū Nuʿaym al-Aṣfahānī, *Ḥilyat al-Awliyā'*, Dār al-Kutub al-ʿIlmiyya, Beirut, 12 vols., 1997 ce.

Aḥmad ibn Ḥanbal, *Al-Musnad*, Dār al-Ḥadīth, Cairo, 20 vols., 1995 ce.

ʿAjlūnī, Ismāʿīl ibn Muḥammad, *Kashf al-Khafā'*, al-Maktaba al-ʿAṣriyya,

Beirut, 1420 ah/2000 ce.

Imām ʿAbdallāh ibn ʿAlawī al-Ḥaddād, *The Lives of Man*, The Quilliam Press, London, 1991.

Bayhaqī, Aḥmad ibn al-Ḥusayn, *Shuʿab al-Īmān*.

——— *al-Sunan al-Kubrā*, Dār al-Fikr, Beirut, n.d.

——— *Dalā'il al-Nubuwwa*.

Bukhārī, Muḥammad ibn Ismāʿīl, *Ṣaḥīḥ*, al-Maktaba al-ʿAṣriyya, Beirut, 1411 ah/1991 ce.

Burleigh, Michael, *Death and Deliverance: Euthanasia in Germany, 1990–1945*, Cambridge University Press, Cambridge, 1994.

Ellis, Albert, *Reason and Emotion in Psychotherapy*, Citadel Press, New Jersey, 1962.

al-Ghazālī, Abū Ḥāmid, *Iḥyā' ʿUlūm al-Dīn*, al-Maktaba al-ʿAṣriyya, Beirut, 1417 ah/1996 ce.

al-Ḥākim al-Nīsābūrī, *al-Mustadrak ʿalā al-Ṣaḥīḥayn*, Dār al-Kitāb alīʿArabī, Beirut, 1990 ce.

Al-Haytamī, Ibn Ḥajar, *Majmaʿ al-Zawā'id*, Dār al-Kutub al-ʿIlmiyya, Beirut, 1408 ah/1988 ce.

Ibn Abī Shayba, *Musannaf*, al-Maktaba al-Imdadiyya, Makka, 1404 ah/ 1984 ce.

Ibn Ḥibbān, *Ṣaḥīḥ*, Mu'assasat al-Risāla, Beirut, 18 vols., 1997 3rd edition.

Ibn Kathīr, *Tafsīr*, 1/311, 587.

Kennedy, Paul, *The Rise and Fall of the Great Powers: Economic Change and Military Conflict 1500–2000*, Unwin Hyman Ltd, London, 1988.

Lawson, Annette, *Adultery: An Analysis of Love and Betrayal*, Basic Books, New York, 1987.

Ibn Māja, *Sunan*, Dār al-Fikr, Beirut, n.d.

Imām Mālik, *al-Muwaṭṭa'*, Dār al-Kutub al-ʿIlmiyya, Beirut, n.d.

Mullen, P. E., 'Jealousy: The Pathology of Passion', *British Journal of Psychiatry*, 158 (1991), 598.

al-Mundhirī, Zakī al-Dīn, *al-Targhīb wa'l-Tarhīb*, ed. Muṣṭafā ʿImāra, Beirut, 1406 ah.

Muslim, *Ṣaḥīḥ*, with Imām Nawawī's commentary, Dār al-Fikr, Beirut, n.d.

Nasā'ī, *Sunan*, Dār al-Kutub al-ʿIlmiyya, Beirut, n.d.

Rogers, C. R., *Client Centred Therapy*, Houghton-Mifflin, Boston, 1951.

———'The Necessary and Sufficient Conditions of Therapeutic Personality Change', *Journal of Consultative Psychology*, 21 (1957).

Stearns, R. N., *Jealousy: The Evolution of an Emotion in American History*, New York University Press, New York, 1989.

Ṭabarānī, *al-Muʿjam al-Kabīr*, Maktabat al-ʿUlūm wa'l-Ḥikam, Mosul, 20 vols., 1983 2nd edition.

Tirmidhī, *Jāmiʿ al-Ṣaḥīḥ*, Dār al-Kutub al-ʿIlmiyya, Beirut, 1408 ah/ 1987 ce.

Irvin Yalom, *The Theory and Practice of Group Psychotherapy*, Basic Books, New York, 1975 (2nd ed.).

INDEX

Abū Bakr, 141
Abbasid caliphate, 132
Abraham, 5
abstinence, 106
Abul-ʿAzā'im, Muḥammad, 45
active/passive dichotomy, 14–15
Adam
  as active pole, 14
  creation of, 6
  Eve created from rib of, 118
adhān, 44
adultery
  prominent in the West, 82
  sign of the Final Hour, 62
aggressiveness, 40
Alī ibn Abī Ṭālib, 26, 150
ʿAmr ibn ʿAbsa, 141
Anas ibn Mālik, 141
angelic inspirations (*ilhāmāt*), 39
Angel of Death, 27
angel(s)
  angelic inspirations, 39
  Angel of death, 24
  Angels of Proximity, 28
  visiting in dreams, 47
anger, 38–39
animals
  created in pairs, 13
  energy spirit of, 33
  in dreams, 50
  meat production, 77
  perception of the world, 37
Antichrist
  appearance of, 87, 91
  claiming to be Christ, 151
  deception of, 91
  description of, 91
  man of darkness, 153
Arafāt, Plain of, 103
archetype
  and Carl Jung, 54, 84, 90
  in Divine Knowledge, 14, 46, 53
  pseudo-archetypes, 54
atrocities
  committed by West, 89
  Muslims cleaner history of, 144
Attributes of God
  as symbols, 6
  Mercy of, 7–8
  nature's dependence upon, 3
  not to be taken literally, 6
  of Beauty, 15

set in pairs, 13
their relation with the Divine Essence, 53
Avicenna, xiv
awe of God, 143
Azrael, 8

balance, quality of, 104
Baldwin, C., 126
banks, 65
baraka
definition of, 11
increased in certain times, 20
relation to time, 19
result of strong faith, 11
Barzakh. See *Intermediate Realm*
beauty
and Paradise, 32
instilling hope, 99
in universal pattern, 54
relation to mercy, 97–98
Beauty
as passive attribution, 14
Beauty (jamāl)
Divine attributes of, 6, 15, 97, 99
behavior
conditioning of, 39, 41
internal dimensions of, 42
Bilāl ibn Rabāḥ, 28
birth
and modern conception of self, 23
calling the adhān thereafter, 44
body
relationship to spirit, 15, 27, 33, 39
Bosnia, 145
breastfeeding, 44
brotherhood, xiv, 111
Caliphate, 136
chaos and order, 56
character
changeable aspects of, 42–43
classifications of, 103–104
developed by ambitions, 45
immutability of, 42
relation to faith, 108, 119
chastity, 88, 106
Chernobyl, 78
childhood
development of intelligence, 44
innocence of, 50
seeing children in dreams, 50
stage of life, 27
China, 130
chivalry, 145
Christianity
decline of, 74
imitation of Christians, 65
replaced by psychoanalysis, 83
chronological succession, 18
chronological succession (*tatabuʿ zamānī*), 18
civilization, Islam as a measure of, 55
clothing
religious significance of, 66
cognition, 35, 40, 97, 149
collective unconscious, 54, 84, 90
colonialism, xii
companions
taught by the Prophet ﷺ, 140
Companions
entrusted with knowledge, 55
and learning virtues, 43
preparing for death, 28
preparing for the Hereafter, 31
seeing them in dreams, 51
compassion of God, 124, 142
confidence in God, 103
contentment, 100–101
continence, 104, 106
counseling, 131–32
courage, 7, 39, 104, 107
creation
interconnectedness of, 3

pairs therein, 13–16
succession of events, 18
crusaders, 144

Dajjāl. See *Impostor*
Daniel ﷺ, 50
darkness and light, 124, 153
Day of Judgement
condition of people therein, 67
relative time therein, 19
death
Angel of Death, 24, 27
aversion to, 68
believers having joyous expectations of, 28
difficult for disbelievers, 28
errant conceptions of, 27
experiencing the invisible realm whereupon, 8
explication of, 122–25
fear of, 123
Intermediary Realm thereafter, 9
painful process, 28
release from constraints of this world, 4
remarriage after loss of spouse, 125
remembrace of, 122
remembrance of, 123
sleep as 'little' form of, 24
visitation of cemeteries, 123
wishing for, 56
deforestation, 76
dehumanizing effects of technology, 127
demons
demonic dreams, 48
worse kind of jinn, 10
deterioration of humankind, 55–57
dhikr as therapy, 132
dignity, 7, 65, 66, 105, 106, 110
dimensions of existence, 3–6
disbelief, 7, 42, 109, 110, 138
discontentment, 101–103
discrimination
prohibition of, 110
disequilibrium, 16, 76, 104
Divine Light, 32, 54
divorce, 114–115, 119–122
dreams
abstractions taking on forms therein, 9
angelic inspiration of, 47
contamination of, 48
demonic inspired dreams, 48
Divinely inspired, 47
Ibn Sīrīn, 49–51
interpretation of, 49–52
ordinary kinds of dreams, 48
perception of time, 18, 19
premonitory dreams, 47
seeing the Prophet ﷺ, 47
symbolism therein, 49–51
veracity of, 49
visions (ru'yā) therein, 47
world of imagination, 10
dressing, 65–66
duration (madda), 17

earthly stage of life, 23
education
of children, 44, 116
of women, 127
psychology, 84
religious education neglected, 127
Western influence of, 80
Western style, xii, 132
ego, 45
dominance of in modern world, 63
evil of one's ego, 136
greater jihād against, 137
incites toward evil, 34
lower thoughts of, 38
relation to soul, 33
tricks of, 137
Einstein, Albert, 78
elders, respect of, 111

elements of personality, 42
Ellis, Albert, 85–86
entertainment, 67
equality, 102–103
euthanasia, 89
Eve, 14, 118
evil eye, 132
evolution, theory of, 85

Fāṭima, 124
faith
  certitude, 105
  effect of on behavior, 10
  perfection of, 108
  relationship with modesty, 105
  trials and tests, 101
  wholesomeness of, 107
false scholars, 59
family
  centrifugal forces of, 16
  choosing a wife, 44
  father the head of, 114
  parenthood, 113–115
  psychotherapy, 131
  religious education of, 118
Farewell Pilgrimage, 20, 55, 119
financial autonomy, 121
fiṭrā, 95
five stages of life, 24
Frank, Jerome, 131
freedom of speech, 61
free will, 85, 86
Freud, 84, 90, 133
frugality, 106
fundamentalist outlook, xii

Gabriel, 8, 9, 10, 19, 112
Geneva Convention, 146
Ghanī, 98
Ghazālī, Abū Ḥāmid, xiv, xvi, 33, 35, 39, 104, 121
Gilligan, J., 88
gratitude, 99, 106, 115
Greeks, utilizing writings of, 132
greenhouse effect, 77
Guarded Tablet (al-Lawḥ al-Maḥfūẓ), 14

habits, 45
Ḥajj
  Farewell Pilgrimage of the Prophet ﷺ, 20, 55, 119
  special time of, 20
  performed on behalf of deceased family members, 115
heart
  between the fingers of the All-Merciful, 7
  center of gravity of the soul, 16
  love of God, 99
  meaning of, 33
  purification, 102
Hell
  representing remoteness from God and mercy, 153
  rigor of, 98
Hitler, Adolf, 89
Hoffman, Gerhard, 89
hope (*rajā'*), 99
horizontal relationships, 15
House of Might (*bayt al-ʿizza*), 5
human rights, 89, 90

Ibn ʿAbbās, 100
Ibn Sīnā, xiv
Ibn Sīrīn, 49, 50, 51
identity crises, 82
ignorance
  darkness of, 153
  intellectual myopia, 23

opposed to knowledge, 13
weakness of faith, 122
ʿIlliyūn (abode in Hereafter), 9
imagination
and dreams, 10
Intermediary Real, 10
related to images and forms, 35
World of Similitudes, 47
Impostor (Anti-Christ), 87, 91, 151, 153
industrialization
altering financial order, 121
uprooting people, 79
infancy, stage of life, 27
inspired intellect, 34
inspired intellect (*al-ʿaql al-mulham*), 34
intercession, 31, 124
Intermediary Realm, (*al-barzakh*) 150
freedom therein, 4
relation to dreams, 47
relation to the soul, 150
spirits abiding therein, 9
third stage of life, 29
Intermediary Realm (*al-barzakh*), 9
interpretation of dreams, 49, 51
inversion of reality, 60, 91
iqāma, 44
Ireland, 80
Islamic psychology, xiv
Islamic psychotherapy, 129–132

Jābir ibn ʿAbd Allāh, 106
jealousy, 48, 81, 82
Jerome, Frank, 131
Jerusalem
Crusaders' slaughter of Muslims therein, 144
Night Journey to, 19
Jesus, 24, 87, 151
Jihād, 135–138
abandomnent of, 68
greater and smaller versions of, 54
outward and inward, 68
rank of, 114
jinn, 10, 37, 132
Joseph ﷺ, 50
Judgement Day
approach of the Hour, 56
Bridge (*Ṣirāṭ*) of, 31
intercession of the Prophet ﷺ therein, 31
major signs of the Final Hour, 69
signs of, 61–62
Judgment Day
minor signs of the Final Hour, 69
Jung, Carl, 54, 84, 90

Kaʿba
relation of to the heavenly realm, 5
spiritual symbolism of, 52
Kennedy, Paul, 74
khalīfa, 57, 63
khawāṭīr (thoughts from lower tendencies), 38
khawārij (renegade group), 146
kinship, 112–13
knowledge
of the Attributes of God, 99
based on revelation, 132
basis of serenity, 101
disappearance of, 62
dissemination of, 138
light of, 153
one's knowledge of God, 97
reduction of to empiricism, 74
revealed knowledge, 83, 107
and sincerity, 108
and *tawḥīd*, 108

language, symbolic use of, 36
Lawḥ al-Maḥfūẓ, 14

Lawson, Annette, 88
Laylat al-Qadr, 5
life's fives stages, 24
light
  and ablution (*wuḍū'*), 124
  as knowledge, 153
  creation of God, 3
  flooding Paradise, 153
  in the grave, 9
  of God, 32, 54
  of good deeds reaching those who died, 30
  pillar of extending to the Divine Presence, 12
  radiating throughout the universe, 53
literalism, 52
Lote Tree, 6, 7, 8, 19
love of God, 39, 99

mad cow disease, 77
Madīna, 6, 32, 47
madness
  covering reason, 10
  invered image of spiritual ecstasy, 151
  psychological maladies of, 130
magic, 132
Mahdī, 69, 70, 153
Majesty
  Attribute of God, 6, 13, 15, 97, 98, 101
Makka, 5, 19, 47, 96, 139
mankind
  decay of, 69
  destiny of, 23–31
  deterioriation of, 55
  given revelation from God, 23, 55
  invited to submit to God, ix
  need for religion, 151
  provided scriptural evidence, 4
  pyschological behavior of, 129–30
manners, 45, 50, 111, 137
marital relationship, 117
marriage
  institution of, 116–18
  marriage rate, 80
  potential difficulty therein, 119
  prohibited for those couple of a common wet-nurse, 44
  qualifications of a marriageable woman, 116
  safeguarding the marital bond, 119
mass indoctrination, 73
maturity
  and marriage, 116
  spiritual, 26
  stage of life, 27
media
  spread of ignorance, xiii, 61
mediocrity, 95, 96
Messengers, ix
Michael, 8
Michael (angel), 8
milk, 44
Milosevic, 89
modernism, 82
modernization
  and deterioriation of man, xi
  critical evaluation of, 152
  dehumanizing effects of, 127
  identity crisis of, 82
  making man as a 'thing', 23
  redefining the role of women, 80
modesty, 105
moral courage, 107
Moses, 143
motherhood, 80, 113
motivation, 34
mourning, 124
Muʿādh ibn Jabal, 28
Muʿāwiya, 141
Muḥammad ﷺ
  compared to a full moon, 54
  Farewell Pilgrimage of, 20, 55, 119

intercession of, 31, 124
Night Journey of, 19
pledge of the Prophet, 25
Seal of Prophecy, 25
vision of in dreams, 47
Mughnī, al- (Divine Name), 98
Mujīb, al- (Divine Name), 98
Mullen, P. E., 81
multidyadic relationships, 16
Munkar, 29
Muslims
adopting ways of the West, 64–65
benefit to society, 126
brotherhood, 110–112
effected by colonialism, xii
first three generations of, 49–50
purification through hardship, 101
treasury of sacred wisdom, xi

Nakīr, 29
nationalism, 139
natural disasters, 101
nature, polution of, 76–78
Neighborliness, 112
Night Journey of the Prophet, 19
Night of Destiny (*Laylat al-Qadr*), 5
nobility, 45, 46, 57, 104, 106
norms, 95–97
nuclear pollution, 78

oil pollution, 78
old age, 27, 69
order and chaos, 56
ozone layer, 77

pairs, 13–17
Paradise
proximity to God, 153
psuedo-paradise of this world, 85
purest form of mercy, 98
parenthood, 113
passive-active dichotomy, 14–15
peace, greetings of, 111
Pen (*Qalam*), 14
perfection
of God, 99, 151
of God's attributes, 15, 54
of human behavior through the Prophet's sunna, 96
relative aspects of, 99
Pharaoh, 143
philosophy, 132
Physical courage, 107
pleasure seeking, 34, 36, 37, 80
political power
deterioration of government, 56–58
political leadership, 63
predators' ego, 45
qualifications of a ruler, 56
polution, 76–78
polygamy, 120
Pool (of the Hereafter), 32
Populous House, 5, 8, 52, 53
Populous House (*al-bayt al-maʿmūr*), 5
predatory characterisitcs, 46
pre-earthly stage of life, 25
premonitory dreams, 47
prevention of illnesses, 130
pride, 45, 105
productivity, 125
Prophets
and the purity of religion, x
dismissed as irrelevant by the Impostor, 88
led in prayer by the Prophet Muḥammad ﷺ during his Night Journey, 19
nearest to earthly perfection, 152
pledging their belief in the Prophet Muḥammad ﷺ, 25

scholars the heirs of, 59
spirits of, 8
suffered many hardships, 101
visions of in dreams, 47
pseudo-religions, 87
pseudo-spirituality, 84
psychology, 83–84
psychotherapy, 129–132
psychotic illness, 41
punishment, fear of, 38

Qalam, 14
qalb. See *heart*.
Qur'ān
preserved verbatim, xi
Qur'ān
a blessing for believers in the Hereafter, 9
and dream interpretation, 50
caused to descend on the Night of Power, 5
children recitation of on behalf of deceased parents, 115
first source of knowledge, followed by the Sunna, 25
incorruptible sacred book, x
last sacred scripture, xi
preserved verbatim, xi
providing (with the Sunna) comprehensive teaching for life, 110
recitation of for a person near death, 124, 125
recitation of for the dead, 30
revelations of about pre-earthly stage of life, 25
use of symbols, 52

Rabb (Divine Name), 151
Raḥīm, al- (Divine Name), 98
Raḥmān, al- (Divine Name), 7, 98
Raḥmāniyya, 7
Rational Emotive Therapy, 85
Razzāq, al- (Divine Name), 98
reason, 34
relationships
active/passive dichotomy, 14
bonds of kinship, 60–61
disruption of, 60
horizontal and vertical, 15
man and Creator, xi
mother and daughter-in-law, 114
multidyadic, 16
reliance on God, 99, 103
religion
birth and death of, x
flow and an ebb, 60
growing weaker with time, x, 55–56
pseudo-religions, 84, 87
science as religion, 84–86
renewers of religion, 70
reproachful soul, 34
reproachful soul (*al-nafs al-lawwāma*), 34
revelation
basis of scriptural evidence, 4
Islam as last episode of, x
knowledge based on, 23, 97, 150
of the Qur'ān, 5
source of is one, xi
Rightly-Guided Caliphs, 42, 57, 63
rights of kinship, 112
rigour, 102–03
Rogers, Carl, 131
ruwaybida, 61

sacred law (*sharīʿa*)
deviation from, 57
differences of among religions, xi
legal systems ignoring of, 64
Muslims urged to followḍ, 58
neglected by rulers, 58
observance of, x, 42, 57
on war, 135–138

regulations relationship between man and Creator, xi
rights of animals, 110
ruler feigning upholding of, 58
saints
mitigating presence of, 11
prayers of, 28
Saladin, 70
Salmān the Persian, 28
Satan
demons, 10
disbelievers as followers of, 10
disobeying God's commands, 6
forces of evil, 54
hosts of, 12
influence of, 37
influence of denied as myth, 90
insinuations of, 38, 151
insinuations (waswās), 38
sees people from whence you see them not, 12
whispering tactic of, 38
scepticism, 85
scholars
corruption of, 65
death of and the dimunition of knowledge, 59
false scholars, 59
formulating Islamic psychology, xiv
heirs of the Prophets, 59
resistance to westernization, xii
those among them who lie, 58
science as religion, 84–87
self-esteem, 102–03
Seraphiel, 8
serene soul, 34
serene soul (*al-nafs al-muṭma'inna*), 34
sexual relations
according to *sharīʿa*, 106
and attire, 105
between spouses, 121–22
chastity demeaned by today's youth, 88
fidelity therein abandoned, 82
marriage, 117
rise of homosexuality, 88
sexual instinct, 106
Sijjīn (abode in Hereafter), 9
sincerity, 108–09
sleep as 'little death,' 24
sleepers in the cave, 20
social manners, 45
social prominence, 46
society
consumption obsessed, 125
degeneration of Muslim societies, 91
destruction of women's role therein, 80
disorder therein, 82
inversion of values, 91
marginalization of moral codes, 82
modern destruction of, 80
Western disruption of, 80
sorcery, 10
soul (*nafs*)
definition of, 33–42
elements of revolving around the heart, 16
harmonization of the elements of, 17
higher than the body, 15
purification through hardship, 101
random quotations about, xiv
soul that incites to evil (*al-nafs al-ammāra bi'l-sū'*), 34
spirit (*al-rūḥ*), 33–42
descent of into the embryo, 24
in the Supreme Company, 8
pre-earthly existence of, 25
seat of, 8
separation of the body at death, 27
spirituality, 91
classification of people according to, 45
in harmony with life's activities, 75
intelligible proof, 86
principles of, 97–103
pseudo-spirituality, 84

usage of the word of, 150
Western civilization severed from, 91
spontaneous sympathy, 26
sports, 67
Stalin, 89
statistics, 95
Stearns, R. N., 82
suicide, 80
Sunna
basing critiques on, 152
clinging to, 59
and clothing, 65–66
comprehensive framework for life, 110
definition of (note), 25
estrangement from, 96
malady of being estranged from, 65
model of, 130
and normative behavior, 95–96
pattern to emulate, 40
perfection of human behavior, 96
source of guidance, 25
symbolism and dreams, 49–51
synthetic perception, 35

tawḥīd
inner unification of, 17
root of a Muslim's dignity, 105
science of, 97
sincerity in, 108
technology
dehumanization of, 75, 127
false hopes of, 69
television, 73, 78
temperament, 42, 46
Terrestrial Heaven (*al-samā' al-dunyā*), 5
terrorism, 136, 142, 143, 146
Throne, Divine
angelic bearers of, 8
Attribute of Total Mercy, 7
cosmological consideration of, 5
description of, 8
and dreams, 47
good deeds ascending to, 12
hierarchical position of, 5
spirits circumambulation of, 53
time, 17–19
time (*zamān*), 17
turban, 65
tyranny
and jealousy, 81
distance of sacred law, 57
sovereignty without solicitude, 152

Uḥud
martyrs of, 30
ʿUmar ibn al-Khaṭṭāb, 26, 42
universe
dimensions of, 3–12
pairs therein, 13–17
time aspects of, 17–20
urbanization
breaking down traditional communities, 82
effect of on families, 114
evils of, 80
usury, 60, 64, 88

values
social, 110–113
spiritual principles, 97–103
veils, 80
vertical relationships, 15
virtues and vices, 103–104
volition, 34

war
defintion of, 135
Geneva Convention, 146
and *jihād*, 135–38
and renegade groups, 146
and sacred law, 142
West

and Westernization, xii
educational system of, xiv
involvement in the Muslim world, xi
Islamic world's reaction to, xii
wisdom
as basic virtue, 63, 104
Divine wisdom, 101
of Prophets and sages, 88
science divorced from, 79
treasury of Muslims, xi
women
active/passive dichotomy, 14
good treatment of, 118
motherhood, 80
role of, 80–82, 117, 118
Western paradigms of, 88
Work Ethics, 125–26
world of imagination (*ʿālam al-khayāl*), 10
World of Similitudes (*ʿālam al-mithāl*), 9-10
wuḍūʾ, 124

Yā Sīn, recitation of, 28
youth, 27

zodiac, 43